D0914378

The Urban Countryside

by Robin H. Best

THE MAJOR LAND USES OF GREAT BRITAIN

THE CHANGING USE OF LAND IN BRITAIN
(with J. T. Coppock)

LAND FOR NEW TOWNS

THE
URBAN COUNTRYSIDE

*The Land-Use Structure of Small Towns
and Villages in England and Wales*

by

ROBIN H. BEST
M.Sc., Ph.D.
*Reader in Land Use and Environmental Studies,
Wye College, University of London*

and

ALAN W. ROGERS
M.A., M.Phil.
*Lecturer in Environmental Studies,
Wye College, University of London*

FABER AND FABER LIMITED
3 Queen Square London

333.7
B561u

First published in 1973
by Faber and Faber Limited
3 Queen Square London WC1
Printed in Great Britain by
Western Printing Services Ltd Bristol
All rights reserved

ISBN 0 571 09961 0

6/14/74

© *Robin H. Best and Alan W. Rogers 1973*

Contents

CONTENTS

Tables

Illustrations

PLATES

FIGURES

ILLUSTRATIONS

ACKNOWLEDGEMENTS

Acknowledgements are made to Aerofilms Ltd. for the use of Plates I–VI: to Bovis – New Homes Division, for the use of Plate VII: to J. Nunn and Sons Ltd., for the use of Plate VIII: and to John Murray (Publishers) Ltd. for permission to use the quotation from *The Town Clerk's Views* by John Betjeman.

Preface

Small towns and villages are as much a part of the country-side as farms, fields and forests; yet small settlements like these form only a minor portion of the whole extent of rural areas. This is hardly to be wondered at, for urban uses are intensive uses of land, whereas many of the main activities in the countryside, like agriculture, forestry and recreation, are, more often than not, very extensive occupiers. Nevertheless, small towns and villages contribute an essential ingredient to the rural landscape and rural economy of England and Wales. Without them the whole character, interest and life of the countryside would be altered beyond recognition.

It is rather unexpected, therefore, to find that so relatively little is known about this important component of the rural scene from the point of view of its land-use structure and composition. This is especially surprising when it is realised that the old-established and traditional rural industries of agriculture and forestry have a wealth of detailed land-use information available for them, stretching back to the nineteenth century, which provides an essential and fundamental body of knowledge on which their present functioning and future development may be soundly based. With small settlements, however, this is not so. They have always been the poor relations where land-use statistics of rural areas are concerned.

The first limited attempt to rectify this situation arose as part of a more widely-based research project, instituted by Professor Gerald Wibberley at Wye College in the early 1950s with the help of Conditional Aid Funds. As part of this work, Robin Best was involved with reviewing the national pattern of land use and, in particular, with making a new estimate of the total urban area. Small settlements, as urban elements in the countryside, figured in the calculation, but lack of statistical data for villages and hamlets prevented much further progress in this subject after the initial research had been carried out.

Even so, the results suggested that there would be considerable interest and value in pursuing the investigation further should this ever prove possible; but it was not until over ten years later that the intention became a practical possibility. In 1967, Alan Rogers came to Wye to carry out research in this field supported by a studentship from the Ministry of Agriculture, Fisheries and Food. And, at about this same period, the first published map-sheets of the Second Land Utilisation Survey, directed by Miss Alice Coleman at King's College, London, were becoming available for several parts of the country. These maps, for the first time, provided a source of fundamental information on land use in small settlements – a sector of the urban area which had been virtually by-passed in official development plans. The 2½ inch scale was large enough to allow, at last, an adequate land-use representation of these small towns and villages in reasonable detail, and it proved quite feasible to measure and abstract the quantitative data required from the published maps. By this means, the primary statistics for analysis were assembled. Indeed, it is not too much to say that, without the cartographic material provided by the Second Land Utilisation Survey, the greater part of the research covered in this book would have been completely impossible.

These basic land-use data were supplemented, however, by important, if less comprehensive, statistical material provided from other sources, and particularly by several local planning authorities mentioned in the text. Outstanding among them was East Sussex, whose county planning officer, Mr. Leslie Jay, was a pioneer in the application of statistical methods in town and country planning. His continued co-operation and advice from an early stage in the present project has been greatly valued. The authors are also indebted to the Ministry of Agriculture, Fisheries and Food and to the Department of the

Environment for much help and assistance, especially in facilitating access to development plan data for small towns. In addition, special mention must be made of Professor David Thomas, who read and commented on parts of the text in its earlier draft form, and of colleagues, particularly Allan Jones and members of the Statistical Unit at Wye, who volunteered much useful advice. Finally, the efficient typing of Mrs. Jane Pryce from mutilated manuscripts has been a most welcome bonus. The later stages of the work and writing were carried out in the Countryside Planning Unit, which was set up in 1970 by the Principal of Wye College, Dr. Harry Darling, with the generous assistance of Cook Trust funds. The intention of the unit has been to focus and consolidate research and teaching in land use, conservation and related topics, and, in particular, to facilitate the initiation and organisation of a new B.Sc. degree in Rural Environment Studies.

The present book, which has been derived from the studies that have been mentioned, is concerned with a quantitative delineation and analysis of the structure and composition of land use in small settlements of under 10,000 population at both a national and regional level. Comparisons of these villages and small towns with cities and more populous urban centres have also been made. Particular attention has been given to the space standards adopted; and, in this connection, the general relationship between size of settlement, indicated by population, and the density of development is closely investigated. As a result, a concept termed the density-size rule has been formulated which gives quantitative expression to the proposition that, as the population size of settlement increases, so the density of development becomes tighter. The influence of settlement function on land-use patterns is also considered, and so are the effects of changes in the economic and social structure of small settlements and the impact of planning policies on them.

From this brief outline of contents, it will be apparent that the book is not intended to be in any sense a 'popular' treatment of the subject of land use in small towns and villages. Rather, the objective has been to provide a detailed, factual statement and analysis of a topic on which a great deal of emotional response exists. Indeed, the text is written particularly, though not exclusively, for the student of environmental studies, geography or town and country planning in universities and colleges of higher education or in sixth forms; for the academic geographer and economist interested in the spatial aspects of urban and rural land use; and for the professional planner who has the unenviable responsibility for determining how and where these small settlements shall develop or change in their physical structure. Most of these groups, and especially the general reader who is less interested in technical detail, may like to refer at a fairly early stage to the final chapter, which provides a statistical summary as a more direct and easily comprehensible guide to the previous text. In line with many professional journals in this broad area of environmental and geographic study, metric measures, and particularly hectares (ha) rather than acres, are used throughout the book. A detailed conversion table for these area measurements will be found in Appendix I.

The individual investigations comprising this comprehensive study have been carried out over a considerable number of years. Now that they have been brought together in an integrated form, it is hoped that they will contribute to a fuller and more accurate understanding of the great range of predominantly rural settlements in which nearly one-fifth of our whole population lives and which occupies a similar proportion of all urban land in England and Wales. Clearly enough, this sector is too substantial and important a part of the total environment to be ignored in any serious assessment of land use in this country.

Wye College R.H.B.
June 1972 A.W.R.

1 · The Countryside and its Settlements

'. . . To consider the conditions which should govern building and other constructional development in country areas consistently with the maintenance of agriculture, and in particular the factors affecting the location of industry, having regard to economic operation, part-time and seasonal employment, the well-being of rural communities and the preservation of rural amenities.'

These terms of reference were given in October 1941 to the members of the Committee on Land Utilisation in Rural Areas. A year later they were to produce one of an important wartime trio of government reports concerned with planning for the post-war period – the Scott Report (1942). As is so often the case with official documents of this kind, the picture which was presented was very much the one that was broadly expected. This is certainly not to suggest that there was any resort to political chicanery. It was simply that, not unnaturally, there was an almost unconcious tendency to reflect the general consensus of the time. In a Britain beset by wartime drabness and deprivation, and under the threat of destructive invasion, a reminder of the apparently tranquil and unsullied countryside and the need to preserve this heritage had an immediate and profound appeal to the whole population.

The townsman's idea of the countryside, often distorted or romanticised, is nevertheless very pervasive. To the most urbanised Englishman, whose family has lived and worked in the town for generations, who has no family ties away from the city, and whose job has no relevance whatsoever to agriculture, the countryside all the same assumes a place in his emotions which would often put to shame the most thorough-going countryman. The countryside stands for all that is important in Britain; it is the expression of the good life away from the stresses and strains of the city and the symbol of everything which is considered truly British. As Nan Fairbrother (1970) has said: 'it is natural for urban people to idealise the country life; indeed it is a measure of our distance from country reality'.

But whether in town or countryside, increasing concern has been shown in the last thirty years for the conditions under which people live. Although complaints are often made about bureaucracy and planning in as much as they are felt to interfere with the rights of the individual, the fact remains that there is greater regard for, and more positive action on behalf of, the welfare of the population than ever before. Social provisions are made for the benefit of each person from the cradle to the grave. Provision is made for his health, his education and his livelihood on a scale unmatched anywhere in the world. And on a wider front, the conservation and improvement of the environment itself are the responsibility of several government departments. Not unexpectedly perhaps, the future of the countryside has assumed an important place in this general concern.

Though possessed of a long ancestry in writing and discussion, a complete programme of social welfare in Britain has only a short effective history of about thirty or forty years. Much of the relevant legislation came after the Second World War, though the actual foundations of the present educational, medical and social security systems date from the wartime period itself. In this respect, it is intriguing to find that in 1942, with peace still three years away, it was also thought expedient and worthwhile to consider, in the Scott Report, the future of England's rural areas and to re-emphasise the importance of the countryside and the need for 'the preservation of rural amenities'. This was at exactly the same time that Beveridge was reporting on the needs for social welfare and security. A quarter of a century later, it is perhaps tempting to express a little surprise at these priorities.

It should not be deduced from these comments that any deprecation is intended of the concern shown for the rural parts of this country: rather the reverse. Nevertheless, it is important to emphasise the warm and sympathetic response which the countryside raises in the hearts and minds of Englishmen if only to point out that a well-intended benevolence and an exaggerated romanticism are no substitutes for accurate factual data, clear thinking, and efficient policies when the practical problems of rural areas and their settlements have to be resolved.

But the inclination to extol the countryside has not always taken a completely impractical form. By the second half of the nineteenth century, the appreciation for natural scenery which had come with the writings of Wordsworth and the Romantics had taken a practical turn in the foundation, for example, of the Commons, Open Spaces and Footpaths Preservation Society in 1865 and the National Trust in 1895. Interest in the economic welfare of rural areas, as well as a care for landscape and amenity, was encouraged by the formation in 1921 of the Rural Industries Bureau, now the Council for Small Industries in Rural Areas. Five years later, in 1926, one of the best-known associations in this field was formed – the Council for the Preservation of Rural England.

As in many other areas, private initiative led the way in the formulation of the first ideas and arrangements for rural planning and amenity conservation, while government action lagged behind. Not until the 1930s was any official move made to legislate for an effective form of town and country planning, and even then rural planning took second place in preference to urban matters. Thus, the Green Belt Act of 1938, which gave some protection to rural areas from the ravages of suburban growth, was conceived not as a positive approach to rural problems but essentially as a means of providing recreational facilities for the metropolis. Later town and country planning legislation, particularly the 1947 Act, continued this urban bias. Only recently have active, practical attempts been made to plan rural areas, though even these are often on an individual, ad hoc, basis.

The Scott Report of 1942, which has already been mentioned, was perhaps the first official attempt to provide a *modus operandi* for countryside planning. Its recommendations and suggestions make familiar reading today for they have continually been echoed in subsequent policy statements at both the national and the local level. The Scott Committee advocated a general improvement in rural housing and services and the encouragement of the urban population to use the countryside for recreational purposes in a wise manner. Industrial development in rural areas was regarded as being desirable to a limited degree only, and additional housing and other building were to be allowed solely by means of a strongly-based planning procedure with due allowance made for the demands of agriculture.

In essence, great weight was given to agriculture as having an all-important and pre-emptive right to the use of the land in rural areas. This attitude of mind was in some respects the result of the terms of reference given to the Committee, but, as we have seen, it was also indicative of the general climate of opinion at the time. However, the members of the Scott Committee were not unanimous on this point of agricultural pre-eminence, and S. R. Dennison appended a minority report which contended that agricultural considerations regarding rural land use should stand on their own merits in particular cases, and should not necessarily take precedence over other factors. His viewpoint would today find far greater acceptance than thirty years ago, and in many ways it is true to say that his recommendations, rather than those of the majority report, have been followed in practice when deciding on rural–urban conflicts of land use in the recent past.

Post-war legislation has to some extent followed the main suggestions put forward by the majority of the Scott Committee. Their demands for an adequate planning procedure for rural areas have been largely met by the provisions of the 1947 Town and Country Planning Act which set up the rudiments of the planning system which operates today. Although criticism of this system rightly points out that it is largely negative in its action, in so far as it seeks to prevent inappropriate development rather than to plan positively for good development, this attitude of stringent control was in many ways the viewpoint put forward by the Scott Report. To return to its terms of reference, it is instructive to note that mention was made of 'the maintenance of agriculture' and 'the preservation of rural amenities' – both phrases reflecting the conservationist and even preservationist approach which influenced the Committee and which has coloured much subsequent legislation.

In many respects the improvement of British agriculture, which was at the centre of the Scott Committee's deliberations, was encouraged not through the medium of rural planning law but through the more direct channels of the 1947 Agriculture Act. Similarly, their recommendations for the preservation of large areas of the country which are of particular scenic value have also been implemented by subsequent government action. The Scott Committee specifically advocated the establishment of National Parks as well as the protection of certain other amenity areas, notably the coastline; and, in 1949, the National Parks and Access to the Countryside Act carried these recommendations into effect. More recently, the formation of the Countryside Commission under the Countryside Act of 1968 has resulted in a widening of functions compared with those of the old National Parks Commission. These are now concerned with the use of rural land, particularly for recreational purposes, outside the boundaries of the National Parks as well as inside them.

Two main conclusions, then, are to be drawn from what has already been said. One is the regard and attachment, which sometimes borders on sentimentality, that a great many townspeople as well as countrymen feel for the British countryside. The other is the way in which this feeling has been give some practical effect in recent years through private organisations and public legislation. But despite this concern, there is considerable apprehension today over the absence of any concerted attempt at countryside planning (R. J. Green, 1971). Fears are expressed which echo those of the Scott Report; fears for the destruction of the rural environment by uncontrolled urban expansion and leisure activities, by air and water pollution from manufacturing industries, and by the possibly deleterious effects of the new agri-

23

cultural revolution arising from the excessive use of pesticides, fertilisers and factory farming methods.

One element of the countryside which is particularly open to urban and technological impacts is rural settlement. The hamlets, villages and small towns of England are often regarded with some justification as being the epitome of the rural landscape, and without doubt they represent much that is considered to be desirable and worthwhile. They are, however, in the anomalous position of finding that the original, basically agricultural, functions which initiated their foundation have been replaced by a new set of pressures, often urban in character, to which they find it difficult to adapt. Modern affluence and personal mobility now allow the urban population to express its feelings for the countryside in forms which must inevitably influence the future of even the smallest hamlet. On the one hand, the most picturesque and attractive villages and small towns are open to invasion from tourists and from aspiring residents with city backgrounds, while the original inhabitants are often all too aware of the fact that their new-found prosperity is largely dependent on a refusal to adapt the fabric of their homes to modern conditions. On the other hand, in the more isolated and unattractive settlements, this same absence of modern amenities acts as a positive disincentive and encourages people to move elsewhere.

The planning framework which has developed in this country in the post-war period has not been too well adapted to meet the new stresses being brought to bear on small settlements in the countryside. Inevitably, rural matters have been tackled through the medium of a physical planning structure biased towards the problems of cities and large towns. Only in the last few years has any noticeable shift in emphasis been discernible towards the formulation of policies specifically dealing with settlements in predominantly rural areas.

One important outcome of this arrangement of priorities has been the absence of objective appraisal and rational policies which, in turn, arise from a general lack of knowledge about land use in small towns and villages. In cities and larger towns, the land-use structure is tolerably well-defined, but, in contrast, practically nothing at all is known about the other end of the settlement spectrum. A real and considerable gap in our information exists here, and, until it is filled, no sound assessment can be made of rural settlements, their needs, and the contribution they can make to modern society. This book attempts, for the first time, to provide such a statistical statement of land-use structure and space provisions in small towns and villages which, it is hoped, will assist in the future planning and management of the country-side.

2 · Definitions and Data Sources

It may at first appear somewhat paradoxical to talk of 'urban' land when considering what is usually referred to as 'rural' settlement. Yet this terminology, which will be adopted in subsequent chapters, is in fact completely logical and reasonable – though a little preliminary explanation may be needed. Just as geographers and planners have often tended to use the designations 'village' and 'town' without defining their meaning or distinguishing between them very clearly, so have they also used the term 'rural' without a proper understanding of what the word entails.

In a land-use context, rural land encompasses areas which are under agriculture, forest and woodland, as well as wild, unutilised tracts in a natural or semi-natural state. Urban land comprises not only the sites of cities and towns with their associated features, like transport land, but also includes villages, hamlets and even individual or isolated dwellings which perform a similar function whether located in town or countryside. It follows that settlements of any size, from the largest city to the smallest hamlet, are all considered to be urban, though this does not mean, of course, that the major differences in their land-use structure are not recognised. It is merely that these differences are treated as variations along a continuum within one major category of land use without any merging into the complex of truly rural land uses.

THE DEFINITION OF SMALL SETTLEMENTS

This study is concerned only with that end of the urban spectrum which consists of the less populous and less sizeable categories of settlements, like small towns, villages and hamlets. Generically, these places can conveniently be grouped together as 'small settlements'. This description is still very qualitative, however, and needs to be given a more precise form.

Inevitably, a certain amount of arbitrary decision must enter into any such definition, and there is also the need to take account of the categories into which data are conventionally collected. It is of little use defining a major category of land use in an essentially theoretical and detached manner only to find that its stated boundaries overlap or under-reach those determined by recognised data sources, so making the collection or comparison of statistics difficult and complicated. With this point in mind, the term 'small settlement' as used here refers only to places of under 10,000 population, following the standard definition adopted by the Department of the Environment (formerly the Ministry of Housing and Local Government). Even within this range, it is clear enough that markedly different types of settlement occur and that subdivision is necessary. It is not suggested that this figure of 10,000 population is in any way significant when it comes to a consideration of land-use structure – indeed, it is very definitely not so – but it simply provides a useful and workable division between those groups of larger cities and towns for which considerable land-use information already exists and the smaller places about which relatively little is known at present.

PROBLEMS OF DEFINITION

A full discussion of the definition of urban land has been undertaken elsewhere (R. H. Best and J. T. Coppock, 1962). But, given the operational definition of this major land use as being the built-up area with its associated open spaces, there remain several general problems regarding the delineation of the overall urban area of any particular settlement.

To start with, it is apparent that the area of the administrative unit in which a given settlement is located must not be taken as delimiting its urban area. The administrative limits nearly always overbound the area of land actually covered by urban uses and are therefore irrelevant in this respect. Also of some importance is that certain land uses, which are nowadays normally classified as urban land, often cannot be treated in this way where small settlements themselves are concerned. The reason is that these particular urban land uses, like airfields, military land, opencast mineral workings and even golf courses, are relatively extensive in character and may, in any case, bear little functional relationship to the settlement they adjoin. Where they occur, they are, as often as not, recent uses which have not developed as part of the settlement itself. In cities and large towns such 'special' uses, as they have been called, can be absorbed within the total urban area without any great difficulty. With small settlements, however, the situation is radically different. The inclusion of an extensive piece of mineral working which is contiguous with the built-up area, for instance, will completely distort some of the resulting calculations of the size and land provisions of a small village. As a result, the composition of the total urban area in small settlements must sometimes be on a slightly different basis from that employed in the study of larger settlement forms. But it is worth emphasising that the significance of these small discrepancies should not be exaggerated, as the number of occasions on which these special land uses actually occur within the ambit of small settlements is relatively infrequent.

There is a second problem of definition in the delimitation of the total urban area of some small settlements. In many cases, the distinction between a small, scattered hamlet and a collection of isolated dwellings is so indefinite that the delineation of an individual settlement must rest finally on an essentially subjective judgement. Again, although the area of house-gardens is nominally counted within the residential area of a settlement, it is sometimes confusing to know how the private grounds of large country houses should be treated. In fact, because these areas are often used for some agricultural purpose (as orchards or grazing land, for example), the extent of very large private grounds must normally be omitted in assessing the urban area of a settlement. The method by which all such land not covered by buildings within small settlements should be treated has been set out as follows: 'the main criterion used to distinguish agricultural land from food-producing land included in the urban area (e.g. gardens, allotments, and small orchards) is whether or not the land is used for *commercial* food production' (Best and Coppock, 1962).

THE COMPOSITION OF LAND USE

For the purpose of comparative study between individual small settlements and with other types of urban area, it is clearly essential that a standardised set of land-use categories should be defined to which all data sources can be related. Since so much of the information on urban land uses has come from planning authorities, co-ordinated by the former Ministry of Housing and Local Government in their production of maps and land-use statistics under the provisions of the 1947 Town and Country Planning Act, it is hardly surprising that the most acceptable and usable form of classification is based on the standard Ministry definitions. A brief outline will be given of these definitions, and then it will be shown how figures from other data sources can be made comparable with them.

The Department of the Environment (Ministry of Housing and Local Government) recognises five major categories of urban land use – net residential area, industry, open space, education and residual uses – which together form the overall or total urban area of a particular settlement.

a) Net residential area
This is the most important urban land use, and it is officially defined in some detail (Ministry of Housing and Local Government, 1955). Put in a briefer form, it may be defined as the aggregate house-plot area plus any small associated open spaces and service roads and paths (Best and Coppock, 1962).

b) Industry

As officially used, the category should refer to manufacturing industry alone. In practice, in the submission of development plans, it not infrequently includes the surface area associated with collieries, gasworks, power stations and other public service industries which are located within the particular land-use carto-gram. However, in the case of most small settlements considered in this study no such discrepancy arises: here, the category relates entirely to manufacturing industry, while statutory undertakings are placed correctly with the residual land uses.

c) Open space

This category officially covers both public and private open space, such as parks, playing fields, recreation grounds, allotments, golf courses, cemeteries, and so forth. In some development plans for large towns, confusion seems to have arisen about the inclusion or otherwise of certain kinds of large open spaces, notably exten-sive common lands, golf courses and race courses. With small settlements these problems are minimal; and, where such large-scale distorting features are occasionally found in association with these places, they have normally been excluded from considera-tion.

d) Education

In practice, this has been rather a variable item as treated in some development plans, with private schools and school playing fields, for example, being included under this heading in certain cases and excluded in others. The official definition, which includes school playing fields and the grounds of educational establishments under this category, has been adhered to when-ever possible in the case of small settlements.

e) Residual uses

These uses refer to the remaining land which makes up the total urban area after the four main urban uses, defined above, have been abstracted. As such, they are often regarded simply as a residual element, although in fact they include a number of important land uses. In detail, they comprise 'railway land, waterways, principal business and shopping use and public buildings, together, where applicable, with mineral workings, derelict land, airfields, government establishments, land used by statutory undertakings, and other miscellaneous uses' (Ministry of Housing and Local Government, 1959). The key words here in relation to small settlements are 'where applicable'. As explained previously, mineral workings, airfields and certain government lands are excluded whenever possible from the land-use schedules of these places because of their distorting effects. In fact, however, these particular uses rarely occur within the urban area of small settlements, so the problem of their definition seldom arises.

DATA SOURCES

Accurate data on the land-use characteristics of settlements of under 10,000 population have only been available since the end of the last war, and, in large part, their collection has been stimulated by the increasing interest in land-use planning following the 1947 Town and Country Planning Act. Nevertheless, what is undoubtedly the major source of urban land-use statistics in this country – the town map survey reports of the development plans instituted by the 1947 Act – is noticeably lacking in its information about small settlements. The wealth of other information provided by these development plans has enabled much work to be carried out on larger urban centres, but similar work on small settlements has been hampered by a serious deficiency of data. Some development plans do, in fact, contain surveys of settlements of under 10,000 population, but these are rather few and far between. Moreover, their inclusion in the first

submission of a plan or a quinquennial review is of itself sufficient to indicate that such settlements possess special characteristics which merit close and relatively urgent attention by
planners. Data for such places are clearly of limited value when
an attempt is being made to investigate the normal rather than the
abnormal situation.

The dearth of data on the land-use pattern of small towns and
villages is a function not only of their relative smallness in size,
and so of their seeming insignificance, but also of their absolute
number. No accurate figures are available on the size of the
universe in this context, but since there are over 10,000 parishes
in England and Wales, the number of small settlements is
probably well over 15,000. An attempt has been made in the next
chapter to arrive at some more accurate estimate. Such a large
total clearly precludes the collection of complete and detailed
land-use data after the style of the development plan town maps,
and so, not unexpectedly perhaps, the data sources available for
the present study are all of a selective nature. Indeed, even if this
were not the case, some form of sampling would clearly be desirable in the interests of economy.

However, it has now proved possible to continue the work on
the land-use structure of small settlements first begun in the
1950s (Best, 1957) primarily because a new set of data has become
available since then. From 1961 onwards, successive maps of the
Second Land Utilisation Survey have been produced under the
direction of Alice Coleman of King's College (University of
London). These maps form the main data source used in this
study, but the information has been supplemented from three
other surveys as well. All the sources used are briefly reviewed
below, and an outline of the land-use categories employed in each
survey is given so that slight differences from the standard,
official definitions just discussed may be noted.

a) Second Land Utilisation Survey

In this survey, maps have been produced at a scale of 1 : 25,000
(surveyed at the 6-inch scale) which show formal land uses, both
rural and urban, classified under 40 headings and divided into

13 major Land-Use Groups (A. Coleman and K. R. Maggs, 1965). Generally, these maps can be taken as referring very approximately to 1961. Of the 13 Land-Use Groups, 5 are of relevance in the study of small settlements, and, in addition, one sub-group, allotments, has been included from Land-Use Group 8 (Market Gardening) as it is normally considered to constitute part of the open space area of urban land. The 5 Land-Use Groups considered are as follows:

(i) Settlement – including both residential *and* commercial land, it should be noted. Houses with gardens, newly built-up areas and caravan sites are all covered. Schools and public buildings have been abstracted as separate items.

(ii) Industry – covering manufacturing industry, extractive industry, tips and public utilities.

(iii) Open space – defined by the Survey as 'tended but unproductive land'. Allotments have been added from Group 8.

(iv) Transport – including port areas, airfields, railway land, etc.

(v) Derelict land – regarding which the Survey comments: 'This category is rather strictly defined as produced by the dereliction and abandonment of land formerly devoted to settlement, industry or transport.'

In practice, some modifications of this basic classification have been necessary for present purposes, quite apart from the inclusion of allotments under open space. For example, the sub-group 'extractive industry' has, in general, not been included in any measurements made for reasons given previously, while areas under public utilities are classed as 'residual' uses. The sampling methods and measurement techniques used in connection with the abstraction of quantitative data for the large number of small settlements covered by these maps are dealt with later.

b) *East Sussex rural settlement survey*

Referring to work produced by county planning authorities in the area of small settlement study, D. R. Mandelker (1962) has said that 'East Sussex stands almost alone in attempting a detailed field investigation of its rural community structure'. This exception to the general situation is largely due to the work organised in the early 1950s by the county planning officer for East Sussex, L. S. Jay. A complete survey was made of the rural settlement pattern as it existed in about 1954, and from the investigation a statistical sample of 39 small settlements was drawn, complete with land-use information (Best, 1957).

Although a little dated now, this same sample has been used where relevant in the present study, not only because of its uniqueness and precision in survey, but also because it shows some special characteristics which were considered worthy of further investigation. Measurements for the sample were originally made from 25-inch plans by planimeter, and so the data can be expected to be of a high standard of accuracy. Eleven categories of urban land use were recognised and these are easily related to the standard Department of the Environment definitions.

c) *Small town map areas*

Although it has been explained that the development plans generally disregard small settlements, some data for small town map areas of under 10,000 population are available. Figures for the four main uses only (residential, industry, open space and education) were compiled in the 1950s for 50 such areas (Ministry of Housing and Local Government, 1959), but these data have not been used in this study as they have been replaced by more complete and up-to-date information on 12 small town map areas for which plans have been submitted fairly recently. M. W. Bruce (1967) considered some of these plans in his analysis of urban land-use changes in the decade 1951–61, and the remainder have been submitted since Bruce's work was completed. In order to keep broadly to the base-date of 1961 for purposes of comparison, particularly with the Second Land Utilisation Survey data in mind, only those small town map areas which were surveyed in the years 1960–1 have been included here.

Despite the small size of the eventual sample and the special characteristics which are often associated with the settlements chosen by planning authorities for survey, it should be noted that the information fills a gap left by the other data sources. This is because small town map areas rarely refer to settlements of under about 3,000 population, whereas the other available data tend to emphasise smaller settlements still. Because of the hierarchical structure of the settlement pattern in the countryside, a simple random sample of small settlements produces comparatively few of those in the larger size groups and a corresponding weighting in terms of the smaller villages and hamlets. Since it is difficult to allow for this bias in a random sampling frame, a suitable solution is to investigate the larger settlements separately.

The 12 small town map areas selected for analysis are detailed in Table 1, and their geographical distribution is shown in Fig. 1. The land-use categories used in these surveys all follow the standard Department of the Environment definitions with the basic division into residential, industrial, open space, educational and residual uses.

Small town map area	County	Population at survey date	Survey date
Northallerton	York (N.R.)	9,800	1961
Witney	Oxford	9,400	1961
Clay Cross	Derby	9,250	1960
Milnrow	Lancaster	8,400	1961
New Mills	Derby	8,185	1960
Biggleswade	Bedford	8,070	1960
Wombourn	Stafford	8,000	1960
Whitworth	Lancaster	7,300	1961
Alnwick	Northumberland	7,280	1961
Whaley Bridge	Derby	5,210	1960
Thornbury	Gloucester	3,198	1960
Dolgellau	Merioneth	2,500	1961

Table 1. Small town map areas, 1960/61

35

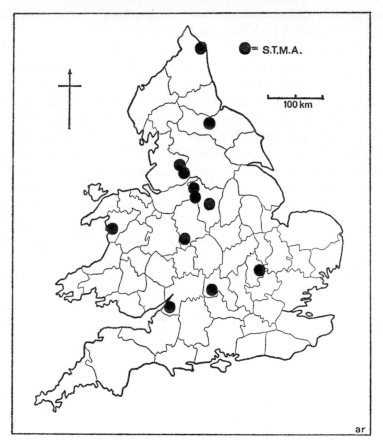

Fig. 1. The distribution of the sample small town map areas, 1960/61

d) Other small settlement data

The deficiency of information on small settlements at the time of the initial researches into the structure of the total urban area in the 1950s (Best, 1957) prompted a supplementation of the figures obtained from East Sussex and the development plans by a limited sample survey carried out with the help of certain county planning departments. This survey was also made partly in order to achieve a better regional distribution of data. Seven authorities were chosen and planning officers were asked to provide land-use information for about 30 small settlements each. In fact, the data collected referred only to the total urban area of the places concerned and the choice of these settlements was largely at the discretion of the county planning officer and was not subject, therefore, to a proper statistical sampling as in the case of East Sussex. The measurement of the urban area by planimeter was also in the hands of persons otherwise unconnected with the study. Nevertheless, there is no reason to believe that there were gross inaccuracies present in the measurements made, as not only were 6-inch maps used but very specific instructions were also given regarding the definition of the total urban area and the general procedure to be adopted. Also, the fear that the settlements were supposedly not chosen by objective means is partially offset by the relatively large number of settlements present in the eventual sample.

In all, the seven selected counties in England and Wales provided data for a total of 213 small settlements. These counties, and the respective numbers of settlements surveyed, were as follows:

County	Number of small settlements
Northumberland	41
Lancaster	36
Monmouth	30
Devon	16
Lincoln (Kesteven)	30
Warwick	30
Oxford	30

COMPARABILITY OF DEFINITION

It has already been explained that the most acceptable categorisation of land uses is broadly that used by the former Ministry of Housing and Local Government and all planning authorities in the preparation of development plans. As in this classification only five major land-use categories make up the total urban area, comparability of data is generally ensured by the amalgamation of several of the more detailed land-use sub-divisions which are used by other sources. In the case of the Second Land Utilisation Survey, for instance, it has been necessary to include the area marked as 'allotments' (Group 8) within the category of open space. Conversely, it has been possible to omit those uses which are not considered to be part of the standard set of definitions. Thus, for reasons already given, areas of opencast and extractive industry have been excluded even though they form part of Land-Use Group 2 (Industry) in the Second Land Utilisation Survey. Land for educational purposes, although technically covered by the settlement category, has also been easily abstracted as a separate item at the $2\frac{1}{2}$-inch scale.

On only two occasions has it been impossible to adapt the data to correspond with the standardised definitions, though in both instances it is certain that this discrepancy is of less significance than it would be if large urban areas were being analysed. The most unsatisfactory disparity is in Land-Use Group 1 (Settlement) of the Second Land Utilisation Survey. This category covers residential, commercial and public building areas, whereas the standard definition is that of the 'net residential area' with the commercial and public building land being classified as residual use. Alice Coleman has explained this situation in the following terms: 'In built-up districts a great many forms of land use are crowded into a small area as compared with the countryside, and there is relatively little space in which to represent them. It was decided, therefore, to associate together as a grey-coloured background all those forms of residential and commercial use which are common to all or most settlements, and vary more according to the settlement's size than to any other factor. This group includes housing, shops, hospitals, churches, business and administrative offices, places of entertainment and so on' (A. Coleman, 1961).

In cities and large towns, the commercial and public building sectors are generally well developed and extensive so that their omission from the Second Land Utilisation Survey maps is an important deficiency. With small settlements, however, this irregularity in definition is not so restricting. In this case, the commercial area is invariably small, even in market towns, while in villages and hamlets such a sector rarely exists at all except as a few separate shops. In addition, the existence of residential quarters above shops in many villages and small towns accentuates the general lack of differentiation between residential and commercial uses.

The second case where it has been impossible to correlate the data sources is in the information provided for East Sussex, which includes some public utility areas (waterworks, local authority depots, etc.) under the industrial category. Properly, this land should be recorded as under residual use for comparative purposes, but, as with the commercial uses, the actual areas involved in small settlements are usually so small that the discrepancy is of little significance.

COMPARABILITY OF DATING

In many ways, it is to be regretted that both the scales and land-use categories used in the First Land Utilisation Survey of L. D. Stamp (1962) and Second Land Utilisation Survey do not allow a detailed comparison to be made between the land-use structure of small settlements in the 1930s and in the 1960s. Indeed, the data currently available for the study of small settlements are so patchy and so recent that time-series analysis is ruled out altogether. It seems that the only way by which any changes could be studied quantitatively would be by a carefully selected sample or by the detailed consideration of a number of case studies.

Although time-series analysis has not been possible, therefore, and the present research has had to be confined to the existing situation, it should not be thought that all the data sources refer to exactly the same base-date. The figures for East Sussex relate to the situation as it existed in about 1954, while both the small town map areas and the Second Land Utilisation Survey are for 1961 approximately. The other local planning authority data for the seven counties in England and Wales broadly refer to 1955. Nevertheless, as a decade easily covers these various years, the small incompatibility in dating is not very important. Moreover, it should be emphasised again that the major source for this study is the Second Land Utilisation Survey and that the other sources, particularly those referring to the 1950s, are only regarded as useful corroborative evidence to be used after the analysis of the major source.

When plans for the Second Land Utilisation Survey were first prepared, the importance of obtaining a synoptic picture of land use was particularly stressed. The initial response to the public announcement in January 1960 of the creation of the survey was so enthusiastic that there is good reason to believe that the first maps produced did attain this goal. However, on a number of the maps which have been published so far, it is clear that the survey work was carried out over a relatively extended period of three or more years. Inevitably, the original surge of activity also fell away somewhat, so that by 1964 about 40 per cent of the country still remained to be recorded in manuscript form. Consequently, the early hopes of a synoptic national picture were not fully realised, and the value of the Survey in this respect has been diminished accordingly.

Even so, on two counts this deficiency is not very serious in the context of the present study. In the first place, the value of the synoptic picture is largely to be found where agricultural land uses are concerned. Here, the recognition of the different crop combinations is at least as important as the simple delineation of the individual crops, and, if the surveying of a land-use map takes place even over two consecutive seasons, the resulting patterns run the risk of being unrealistic. With urban land use in small settlements, however, changes between consecutive years, while they may occasionally be important individually, will hardly effect any conclusions when sample means are considered. Moreover, since all the sample settlements were taken from the first selection of maps to be surveyed and published, the correspondence of the maps with the base-date of 1961 was far greater than with those which will eventually complete the Survey.

PRELIMINARY ANALYSIS OF DATA

Despite the potential vagaries of measurement resulting from the human element and the differences of scale between the various source maps, there is every reason to suppose that the data used in this study have a high degree of accuracy. All the statistics deriving from the three minor data sources were measured either from 6-inch maps or 25-inch plans, and these large scales certainly reduce the possibility of errors and inaccuracies arising. Although the data from the major source, the Second Land Utilisation Survey, were derived from smaller scale, $2\frac{1}{2}$-inch maps, the measurement was done personally by one of the authors and was therefore closely controlled. Cross-checks with some small settlements which were duplicated in the other data samples showed a high degree of statistical correspondence.

Although the Second Land Utilisation Survey attempts to show land use in this country as it existed in the early 1960s, publication of the maps has inevitably been slow. By the end of 1967, when this present study commenced, only 78 maps were available for use out of an eventual total of 843 for England and Wales. Of these 78, five maps were considered to be outside the scope of a small settlement study since they were completely covered by large urban areas and contained no small towns or villages.* The location of the remaining 73 maps is shown on Fig. 2.

It was clear from the outset that, when dealing with a universe of settlements which is probably well in excess of 10,000, the only approach possible was one involving the statistical selection of a representative sample. As no more than a fraction of the eventual total of maps was available for the study, there was clearly a problem regarding sample representation. The only observable bias in the distribution of the 73 maps was that a comparatively large number was found in South Wales and Yorkshire. When using simple random samples, this tended to weight the

* The five maps are: South London (205); Bexley (206); City of London (224); London North (244); Tyneside (815).

results geographically to the detriment of settlements in the eastern and southern parts of the country. Accordingly, it was concluded that some form of simple stratification was needed, and

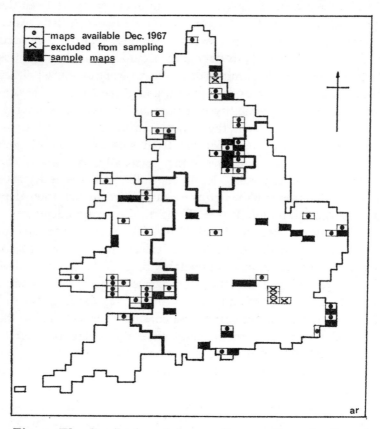

Fig. 2. The distribution of the sample maps from the Second Land Utilisation Survey. The Highland/Lowland division is shown by the heavy line

to this end a division was made between the so-called Highland and Lowland Zones. There was, in fact, a precedent for this process since such a division had been used previously in work on small settlements (Best and Coppock, 1962). Nevertheless, at this stage in the work, it should be noted that the division was made solely with the intention of combatting the statistical bias and not for the purpose of regional analysis.

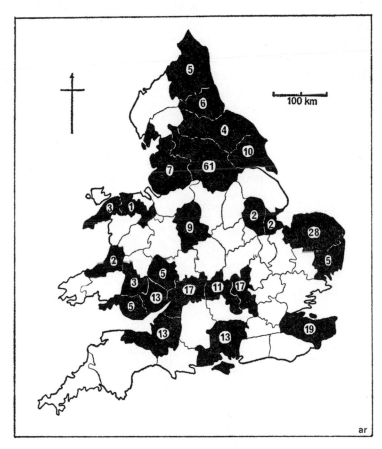

Fig. 3. The distribution and numbers of small settlements in the Second Land Utilisation Survey sample by counties

The division was made broadly following the county boundaries first used by one of the authors (Best, 1957), but these administrative limits were rationalised to follow the map borders (Fig. 2). Of the full total of 843 maps for England and Wales, if a complete coverage had existed, 391 were judged to fall within the

43

Highland Zone and 452 in the Lowland Zone. A sample of 30 maps was drawn, as this number not only provided an adequate array of small settlements for statistical analysis, but was also the largest possible number that could be analysed within the limits of available time and cost. Therefore, the 30 land-use maps out of the 73 available were obtained by sampling with random numbers with the objective of drawing national and regional conclusions which would be statistically valid. The sampling fractions are shown below:

	Highland Zone	Lowland Zone
Full complement of maps in each zone	391	452
Ratio	1	1·156
Available maps in each zone	45	28
Sample sizes for each zone	14 (13·91)	16 (16·08)

These 30 maps, together with the individual totals of small settlements which each map contains, are detailed in Table 2. The

Highland Zone		Lowland Zone	
Barry	5	Shanklin	5
Newport (Mon.)	10	Bournemouth	2
Abergavenny	6	Southampton	6
Monmouth	7	Folkestone	2
Aberystwyth	2	Cheddar	13
Capel Curig	3	Deal	17
Pentrefoelas	1	Thame	19
Hemsworth	15	Chesham	9
Castleford	17	Gloucester	15
Sherburn-in-Elmet	15	Thetford	6
York, West	18	Methwold	5
Lancaster	7	Lowestoft	11
The Hartlepools	6	Downham Market	11
Blyth	5	Crowland Fens	4
		Stafford	9
		Elvington	10

Table 2. Second Land Utilisation Survey – sample maps and small settlement numbers from each map

distribution of the chosen sample is seen from Figs. 2 and 3, the latter showing the distribution of the small settlements by counties.

THE MEASUREMENT OF LAND USES AND POPULATION

The five major land-use categories were measured for each settlement from the 2½-inch Second Land Utilisation Survey maps by the use of a planimeter and a squared-paper grid. The grid was used particularly for the smaller areas of urban land where the planimeter was likely to be somewhat less accurate, and by this means it was possible to make an assessment of any area, in hectares, to one place of decimals.

The problem of distinguishing the boundaries of any particular settlement rarely arose, despite the fact that relatively few settlements are truly nucleated in form. Some strongly linear villages in the Fenland area presented some difficulties of definition, as did certain other loose agglomerations of houses, but in all cases it was possible to delimit boundaries for the settlement which took account of the population enclosed within the urban area. Occasionally, where individually named settlements were joined up in a single urban mass with a total population still below 10,000, such an area was considered as a single entity rather than dividing it by artificial administrative boundaries. Some residential areas which were slightly separated from the main nucleus were counted in the urban area, not only because they clearly belonged to the main settlement, but also because it was impossible to estimate the size of their individual populations, and so subtract these from the main total. Regarding industry, only those sites which were truly part of the small settlement, in so far as they were adjacent to other measured urban uses, were counted.

This process of measurement, then, gave data on the land-use structure of small settlements in the sample, but to gain reasonably satisfactory figures for the corresponding provisions of land under various uses (see Chapter 4) some further modifications were needed. The first necessity was to compile suitable population figures for each settlement. Ideally, such figures are best obtained from a special house-to-house count as was carried out in the East Sussex rural settlement survey. This approach was clearly impossible in the present study since such a count would not only involve disproportionate expenditures of time and labour, but would in any case be practically impossible, as figures were needed for the base-date of 1961 and not for the year of research activity. In the event, the only suitable source was the 1961 Census of Population which was coincidentally, but conveniently, carried out with the same base-date as the land-use survey. However, published Census data are only available for parishes (or wards) and not for individual settlements within each parish. Consequently, it was sometimes necessary to consider several areas of urban land located within a single parish (or ward) as one, individual 'small settlement' rather than as several units. As a result, 488 separate urban units were amalgamated to form 261 'small settlements' for the purposes of analysis. On only one occasion, because of relatively rapid urban extension near the time of survey, was it found that the delineated area of urban land did not correspond fairly accurately with the population census figures. Accordingly, the village in question was omitted from the analyses involving population computations for land provisions, though it was included when estimates of the absolute area of small settlements were made.

A second drawback of the parish population figures was that they also included the population living in isolated dwellings outside small settlements. It has been estimated that about 25 per cent of the population found in all forms of settlement under 10,000 population is located in isolated dwellings (Best and Coppock, 1962), so theoretically it would have been possible to subtract 25 per cent of the total parish population to leave the remainder as an estimate of the people living in small towns and villages. But, in fact, the resulting figure would be a very rough estimate rather than a reasonably correct total, and so some other method of calculation was necessary. Therefore, the adjustment

46

for isolated dwellings was made by multiplying the number of separate houses as portrayed on the land-use map by a factor chosen to represent the average size of household. Several versions of such a factor were available, as the mean household size varies both regionally and temporally (J. B. Cullingworth, 1960). The most suitable figure was to be found in the analysis of the 1961 Census for England and Wales (Housing Tables), where the mean size of household for Rural Districts is given as 2·13 persons per household.

A further adjustment was necessary for hospitals, children's homes and other institutions which were situated well away from the main settlement, but whose population was inevitably counted in the parish total. The irregularity was allowed for by using the Census enumeration for 'population in private households', since this figure excluded the inmates of such institutions. The previous modification for isolated dwellings was then carried out. If such institutions were actually located within the limits of a small settlement, however, the people involved were, of course, included in the final total used.

The results of the land-use measurements and the population calculations outlined above for the individual small settlements contained in the Second Land Utilisation Survey sample are recorded in full detail elsewhere, as are the data for the small town map areas which were analysed (A. W. Rogers, 1969). Similar information for land use and population in the individual small settlements comprising the sample for East Sussex is also detailed in another source (Best, 1957).

3 · Land and Population in Small Settlements

The English countryside with its small towns and villages has for long been a source of great interest to the general public as well as to the academic geographer and the professional planner. Too often, however, such fascination has taken the place of informed and unemotional observation, with a resulting picture of rural conditions which is unduly romantic or else comically rustic. As W. G. Hoskins has said: 'Either it is to be incest in the woodshed and Cold Comfort generally, or it is a kind of Pastoral Mania.' Indeed, almost paradoxically, the writings of Cobbett, Defoe and Celia Fiennes some two hundred years ago are often more informative regarding rural and urban land use than the whole mass of so-called 'topographical' writings which have appeared in the last century and a half.

The lack of objectivity so frequently met with in many works on rural subjects is paralleled by sweeping observations on the supposed character of settlements in the countryside. For example, although the conventional categories comprising rural settlement, like the hamlet, village and small country town, seem reasonably distinct, very little attempt has been made to distinguish clearly between them (but see J. A. Everson and B. P. Fitzgerald, 1969). Again, with the exception of conditions in the mining and industrial villages of the nineteenth century, which are not in the traditional mould of the English rural scene, it is almost universally proclaimed that country living is the good life, despite the shortage of detailed studies on the true nature of rural housing, and social conditions generally, and the complete absence of any basic groundwork on the land-use patterns and densities which exist in small settlements. The present study should go some way towards remedying certain of these deficiencies by the analysis of the sample data which were outlined in the last chapter.

A HIERARCHY OF SETTLEMENT SIZE

The considerable dependence of small villages on the socio-economic facilities provided by larger centres is naturally linked with the existence of a hierarchy of settlements such as that postulated first by Auerbach (1913) and later elaborated by Christaller (1933/1966). Smailes (1946) and, more recently, Smith (1968) have attempted to trace the existence of an urban hierarchy in this country, using indices of status compounded from various service functions performed by large settlements of generally above 10,000 population. Although the present study has omitted any detailed investigation of the service functions of small settlements, a simple analysis of the size of the settlement, in terms of land area, can nevertheless give an indication of its regional standing as a market centre. Since the only work dealing with rural settlement hierarchies in Britain has been in the nature of case studies from specific areas (e.g. H. E. Bracey, 1952 and 1962), it may perhaps be suggested that the national relevance of the sampling frame outlined in the previous chapter provides an initial attempt at filling the gap.

If the 261 small settlements obtained from the sampling of the Second Land Utilisation Survey maps are ranked in terms of their total urban area, and the respective numbers of settlements in each size grouping are plotted as in Fig. 4, a clear indication of the existence of a rural hierarchy is given. As with most of the distributions encountered in this field, the histogram is very definitely skewed in a positive direction from the mean, in this case indicating the greater number of hamlets and small villages, covering less than about 15 ha, when compared with the numbers of small towns. In fact, over half of all the sample settlements have a total urban area of less than 20 ha and over one-quarter

49

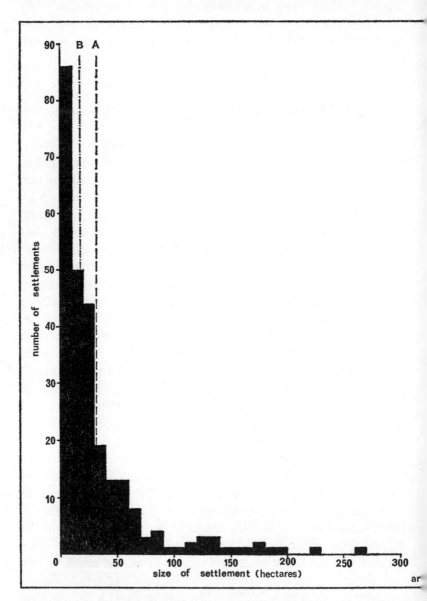

*Fig. 4. The statistical distribution of the total urban area from the
sample small settlements (2L.U.S.): A=mean; B=median*

cover less than 8 ha. However, it should be remembered that, because of the need to amalgamate the settlements found in any one parish (see Chapter 2), this distribution may be a little misleading. While certainly representing the *relative* nature of a supposed hierarchy of settlements, it misrepresents to some extent the *absolute* size of the settlements concerned. This discrepancy is most clearly seen in the comparison of calculated means. The mean size of the total urban area as calculated for the 261 small settlements used in the subsequent analysis is 31·6 ha, whereas the figure for the 488 individual settlements compounded to form the sample of 261 works out at 16·9 ha.

A clearer indication of the 'average' characteristics of small settlement size can be obtained from the median rather than the mean size of the total urban area, simply because the excessively skewed nature of the distribution makes the arithmetic mean a somewhat artificial statistic. Computed for the partly aggregated 261 small settlements, the median size is 17·4 ha, whereas it amounts to under 8 ha for the 488 individual settlements – indicating, as expected, that rural settlement in England and Wales is characteristically made up of very small units.

The land-use composition of these very small settlements is dealt with in greater detail later, but at this point it is interesting to note a further result of the preliminary analysis mentioned above. This concerns the category of open space which generally forms the second most important use of land in small settlements after the residential area. Twenty per cent of the small settlements in the sample had no recorded open space at all, and, if these are included, nearly 60 per cent of all settlements had only 1·6 ha or less of open space contained in their urban area. It should be realised, of course, that in a few cases it is possible that the Second Land Utilisation Survey recorded areas of land as heath or grassland which might more correctly have been termed open space. Nevertheless, it is perhaps instructive to note that the median area of open space found in the sample small settlements (that is, the area which might be considered most characteristic) is calculated as 1·2 ha – a figure which Hoskins and Stamp (1963) in their study of common land cite as being the mean size of village greens in

England and Wales. While it is not suggested that there is any close relationship between these two figures, the information from Hoskins and Stamp not only reinforces the evidence already given for the the generally limited size of small settlements in this country, but also suggests the importance of village greens in making up a large proportion of the 'urban' open space in the countryside. It is, perhaps, a rather more debatable point as to whether the regional differences in open space area and provision which are indicated later are linked to the distribution of village greens as plotted by Hoskins and Stamp.

TOTAL AREA OF SMALL TOWNS AND VILLAGES

The total area under small settlements in England and Wales was originally calculated as 290,078 ha for 1951 (Best, 1957). The method used in arriving at this estimate was based on multiplying the total number of people living in the relevant settlement category (with due allowance made for isolated dwellings) by the density, or land provision per thousand persons (abbreviated to ha/1000p), at which this population was accommodated.* While this evaluation provided the only way to judge the real importance of small settlements as an urban category, the extrapolation of the estimated sample density figures to refer to the whole country had its pitfalls, since so much depended on the accuracy of the original data.

If the 1961 population is used and the same method employed to calculate the total area of small settlements, but using the density or land provision figures calculated for the present study (Chapter 4), the total area obtained is 285,104 ha. The disadvantages present with the direct application of this density technique are immediately apparent for, if this estimated area is correct, it implies that there was an actual loss of urban land, as far as small settlements are concerned, over the period 1951–61. Such an out-

* For a full discussion of these terms and the notation employed see pages 66–8.

come is untenable, so it must be concluded that, either the method of calculation is not robust enough, or else the estimates themselves are not entirely adequate.

While it is quite possible that the technique itself could be at fault when a fairly high level of accuracy is desired, there is additional reason to believe that the estimate for the total area of small settlements in 1951 was probably exaggerated to some degree. Two density or land provision figures were used in the initial calculations. These were for the Highland and Lowland Zones and worked out at 30·5 ha/1000p and 41·9 ha/1000p, respectively. The corresponding figures from the present research are 28·7 ha/1000p and 38·8 ha/1000p – the latter figure for the Lowland Zone showing a notable contrast with the 1951 figure. It may be, therefore, that the 1951 estimates of land provision were on the high side, particularly for lowland England, and consequently the eventual estimate of the total area was probably also too high.

If the more precisely determined 1961 figures for land provision are used in association with the 1951 population, then the revised total area for small settlements at that date becomes 269,938 ha, or some 20,000 ha less than the original statistic. Although this figure is more realistic, the implication still remains that the annual net gain for the period from 1951 to 1961 was only about 1,500 ha. This area is almost certainly an underestimate and again illustrates some inadequacies in the method.

It is clear, then, that the density technique as used above can have serious weaknesses when employed for assessing *changes* in land use, particularly when comparisons are made over short periods. Even so, some tentative conclusions are possible, if the figures are treated with caution. From the evidence available, it seems that the total area under small settlements in England and Wales in 1961 was probably around 285,000 ha. The total extent of urban land in the same year was approximately 1·5 million ha, so that small settlements made up nearly 19 per cent of the whole area. If isolated dwellings and other urban land in the open countryside, like roads and railways, were to be added to this figure for small towns and villages, then about half of all urban land in England and Wales would be accounted for. Such a statistic emphasises only too clearly the considerable importance of the urban sector in predominantly rural areas.

TOTAL NUMBER OF SMALL SETTLEMENTS

There is no single inventory which lists the exact total of settlements of under 10,000 population in England and Wales. Most estimates depend on a knowledge of the number of parishes in the two countries, from which the relevant figure is derived by rough calculation and inspired guesswork. Thus, W. P. Baker (1953) has commented: 'Ten thousand villages in England and all different.' The true figure is greater than this, not only because it must encompass Wales as well as England, but also because it should include *all* agglomerations of houses and associated urban land from the market town to the smallest and most insignificant hamlet, and not just the village.

An attempt can be made to remedy this shortcoming in the light of the present investigation, although the conclusions reached must be as tentative as those regarding the total area covered by small settlements. A number of approaches are possible, the most obvious being a consideration of the aggregate area as previously estimated and the mean size of settlement. In this instance, interest is not centred on the 261 units of the small settlement category used for the main analysis, but rather on the 488 integral parts of this sample. This is because the latter number refers to the full range of individual settlements and includes, at the bottom end of the scale, collections of houses which are no more than small hamlets. If the total area covered by all small settlements is taken as 285,000 ha and the mean size of settlement as 16·9 ha, then the total number of small settlements is estimated as 16,870, or approximately 17,000. If a similar calculation is carried out using the population totals and means of small settlements rather than the land area, then the corresponding figure is 16,950, or extremely close to the previous estimate.

Although, as clearly indicated already, a direct count of all small settlements in England and Wales has not been made, figures do exist for some separate counties where planning officers have been especially concerned with rural planning. Generally, these figures relate only to villages and neglect the small hamlet as an individual entity. In the case of East Sussex, however, where 240 small settlements are recorded, the coverage is likely to be complete. At this rate of occurrence, and bearing in mind the density of small settlements over the whole area of East Sussex, the total for England and Wales may be estimated again at just under 17,000.

Naturally, a precise conclusion on this matter is difficult and is perhaps somewhat academic anyway. But a total of about 17,000 may well be a reasonable estimate for all small settlements, while the number of villages alone, as the more generally recognised basic unit of rural settlement, is clearly less than this.

POPULATION CHARACTERISTICS

As well as giving data on the land-use characteristics of small settlements in England and Wales, the Second Land Utilisation Survey sample can help to provide useful information on population characteristics. Population figures adapted from the 1961 Census are, of course, needed at a later stage in the analysis when the question of land provision or density is considered, but such figures are also of interest in formulating concepts about the basic structure of settlement in this country. Not surprisingly, perhaps, one of the most obvious findings from the analysis of population is a re-statement of the hierarchical pattern already discussed. Fig. 5 should therefore be compared with Fig. 4 as it portrays the distribution of sample settlement sizes, not from the viewpoint of land area, but by a consideration of population totals instead.

This hierarchical distribution is a product of settlement foundation and general population increase over many hundreds of years. At what period the basic structures of land use and population appeared is uncertain, but it would seem that some of these characteristics have not changed a great deal since at least the seventeenth century. Laslett (1965) cites the case of Wingham in Kent as one of the few examples of a single parish for which there

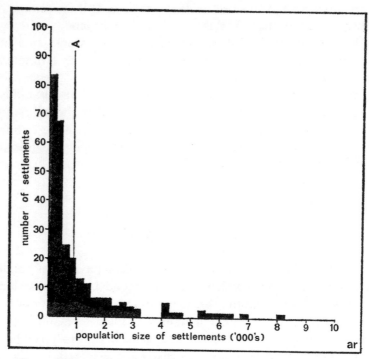

Fig. 5. The statistical distribution of population size from the sample small settlements (2L.U.S.): A=mean

are accurate historical data relating to population and settlement size – in this instance dating from 1705. At that time, the total population was recorded by the local vicar as being 6,411, distributed between 40 centres, and giving a mean settlement size of 160. But this last figure is misleading as the main settlement of Wingham itself had a population of 1,172 which must have made it an important local centre. Purely by chance, this same settlement was one randomly selected in the present sample, and it is interesting to note that the calculated population total for 1961 was 1,378, showing the relatively small amount of growth that has occurred in the last 250 years, most of it probably being fairly recent.

Laslett provides other evidence to suggest that the mean settlement size in the early eighteenth century was somewhere in the range 250–450, based on the number of people recorded by Gregory King (1696) as living in villages and hamlets in 1695 and on the probable number of rural parishes. This population range is not substantially different from the results obtained in the present study, the mean population for the 488 individual settlements being 486. A century or so after the records of Gregory King, at the time of the first national census, the mean size of rural settlement was estimated as 422, based on a random sample of 522 named places (P. Laslett, 1965). Again, this figure corresponds well with the 1961 estimate, allowing for some general growth especially in recent years. Some doubts are raised regarding the nature of Laslett's 1801 sample, however, as he mentions that the median figure for population is as high as 615. When compared with the computed mean, this suggests that his sample exhibits a distribution with a negative rather than a positive skewness. Such a result indicates that there may be over-representation of the larger settlements which would effectively increase the mean value. This impression is reinforced by a more detailed consideration of the statistical distribution. Laslett calculates that only 35 per cent of the 1801 rural population dwelt in settlements smaller than 400 people, while 32·5 per cent lived in settlements of more than 1,000. Even taking the population of the 261 amalgamated settlements in 1961, rather than the full 488 used here, the figures are 50·2 per cent and 25·6 per cent, respectively, suggesting strong over-representation of the larger settlements by Laslett.

Evidence from Gregory King's survey of 1695 also provides material on the total rural population around that date, and again some comparisons are possible with present day conditions. King's figures for the basic population structure of England and

Wales at the end of the seventeenth century are briefly outlined below:

London	530,000, or 10 per cent of total population
Other cities and market towns	870,000, or c. 16 per cent of total population
Villages and hamlets	4,100,000, or over 74 per cent of total population

For present purposes of estimating the total population living in settlements of under 10,000 people, there is need to refer to the last entry (villages and hamlets) and to a proportion of the figure for other cities and market towns. A breakdown of the latter category gives the following population distribution:

4 centres (probably Bristol, Norwich, York and Southampton)	at c. 25–30,000 each
10 centres	at c. 18,000 each
30 centres	at c. 2,200 each
100 centres	at c. 1,300 each
250 centres	at c. 900 each
400 centres	at c. 650 each

Clearly, the last four items are of relevance and are probably as near as it is possible to approach to the theoretical limit of 10,000 persons. This sector contains 681,000 people, a figure which, when added to the population living in villages and hamlets, gives a total of 4,781,000, or just under 87 per cent of the total population of England and Wales at that time.

Two hundred and fifty years later the position has changed completely. A combination of rapid expansion in urban population coupled with much slower rural growth, and even depopulation on occasion, has effectively altered the situation to the extent that the rural/urban ratio is now reversed with some 80 per cent of the population at present living in administrative urban areas. It is possible to calculate approximately the total population living in small settlements of under 10,000 population by taking into consideration the population of all Urban Districts under 10,000 population and the population of Rural Districts, less 25 per cent to allow for people living in isolated dwellings (Best, 1957). The total obtained in this way is about 8,240,000, which was 18 per cent of the total population of England and Wales in 1961.

4 · Land-Use Structure and Space Provision

Though dear to the heart of the topographer, English rural settlement often proves a disappointment to the urban geographer. It shows few of the distinctive features of urbanisation – central business districts, industrial zonation, complex transport networks and the like – which characterise large towns and cities. The general impression is frequently one of structural uniformity. For the social geographer, too, the village has only recently become a point of interest. It is mainly in the present century, with the growth of rural residential estates and council housing, that the old social order, again exhibiting a general consistency of character, has been complicated by an influx of new social groupings with their associated behaviour patterns.

This supposed uniformity has, in part, been the reason why the land-use patterns of rural settlements have generally received scant attention from geographers and economists. A contributory factor, of course, has also been the lack of quantitative data on the subject. Conversely, there has existed a relative wealth of such information for larger towns and cities. Not surprisingly, therefore, it is in this sector that the main work has been done in settlement geography. Land-use models, such as those of Burgess (1925), Hoyt (1939) and Harris and Ullman (1945) have invariably been constructed from examples drawn from populous urban centres, and therefore refer back to cities and large towns when land-use structure and settlement growth are being considered.

In contrast, little attempt has been made to construct a land-use model for rural settlement. The problems involved would make such a task far more difficult than the construction of a model for city land use where economic forces are so often the all-important common denominator. So multifarious are the factors contributing to the urban land-use pattern in rural areas, however, that even the most all-embracing model would inevitably have a low predictive value.

COMPOSITION OF THE URBAN AREA

The apparent uniformity of much rural settlement is immediately evident from a study of the composition of the urban area of small settlements in England and Wales. The data are shown in Table 3 and also in diagrammatic form in Fig. 6.

As might be expected, a large part of the urban area in villages and small towns is taken up by housing. Because the average conditions, with the exception of the small town map area data, usually refer to villages with a mean size of about 1,000 people, it is hardly unexpected that over three-quarters of their land is used for residential purposes. These settlements generally lack the strong industrial base and the notable proportions of transportation and public utility land which characterise larger settlements. Often their only major function is the accommodation of people, while the provision of employment, with all its associated infra-structure, assumes a much lesser role.

Not only is this true of manufacturing industry, but it applies to the service element as well, which is also frequently at a minimum. Commercial land probably takes up less than 5 per cent of the urban area in the average small settlement for, although the main data source in this study does not distinguish this land use separately, a comparison with the figures for East Sussex suggests a percentage which is certainly no greater than this. In the vast majority of small settlements, considering median rather than mean size, the commercial land area is probably a good deal smaller, and may include only one or two shops which are themselves also the residences of their owners. Land used for education is similarly on a minor scale. Schools are generally small, and are frequently without the playing fields which normally form a large

	Average population	Housing	Industry	Open space	Education	Four main uses	Residue
				per cent*			
Second Land Utilisation Survey, 1961 (260)	909	79·3†	3·6	11·4	2·0	96·3	3·7
East Sussex small settlement survey, 1954 (39)	1,053	72·7	2·1	14·1	4·9	93·8	6·2
Small town map areas, 1960/61 (12)	7,216	45·3	9·0	15·0	5·9	75·2	24·8

*Of total urban area   † Including commercial land

Table 3. The composition of the urban area in small settlements. Sample numbers of settlements are given in brackets in Tables 3 to 6

proportion of land under education in larger settlements. Indeed, schools may even be non-existent when educational facilities are

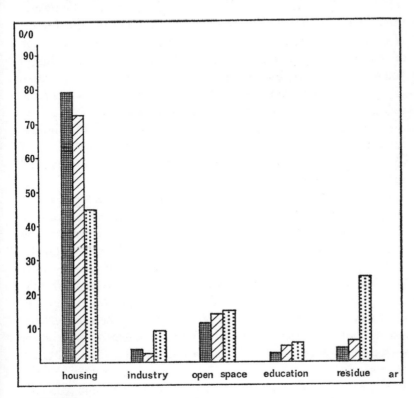

— Second Land Utilisation Survey
— East Sussex Data
— Small Town Map Areas

Fig. 6. The proportionate composition of the total urban area in small settlements

provided in nearby towns. The higher figure for East Sussex reflects the rather larger mean size of settlement in that county.

As with larger settlements, open space provides the second most important use of land in small settlements (discounting the

63

composite category of residual uses in small towns), covering something between 10 and 15 per cent of the urban area. In a sense, this figure is somewhat misleading as it gives little idea of the importance which this use plays in the life of the inhabitants of a small settlement. In large towns and cities, the proportion of land under open space can certainly give some indication of amenity conditions, but this is not so where hamlets and small villages are concerned. In these cases, only the village green, recreation grounds and other formal open spaces go to make up the estimated 10–15 per cent of the urban area, while the population, more often than not, also has direct access to large areas of the countryside which fulfil the same function as the recorded urban open space areas.

Returning to the major use of land in small settlements, housing, it is now possible to make some comments on the various elements which comprise this category. In the first place, the exact content of the residential area as defined here should be emphasised again, as it is clear that only part of the so-called 'housing' area is in fact covered by dwellings. Service roads and some small open spaces are included in this area, but even more important is the land under gardens. Although there is perhaps a danger of romanticising English rural settlement in association with ideas of country gardens and rose-covered cottages, there is at least some supporting statistical information on this subject, even if it is now rather dated. A survey instituted by the Ministry of Agriculture and Fisheries in September 1944, in an attempt to assess the food potential of gardens under wartime conditions, showed the contrasting importance of gardens in urban and rural areas. Of the sample of 3,190 houses investigated, 38 per cent of those in urban areas did not have gardens, whereas the corresponding figure for Rural Districts was only 9 per cent. Interestingly enough, a far higher proportion of urban gardens, where they existed, were left uncultivated (Best and Ward, 1956). Dudley Stamp estimated from his investigations for the First Land Utilisation Survey of Britain that 'broadly speaking . . . in the . . . open type of village and town the amount of land, even under wartime conditions of intensive cultivation, actually under fruit,

I. Blanchland, North-
umberland. An un-
spoilt village, planned
in the early 18th
century, with a layout
which follows the ground
plan of monastic build-
ings dating from the
12th century. Its small
size and compactness
can be seen by com-
parison with the foot-
ball pitch in the
foreground.

Aerofilms Ltd.

II. Juniper Hill, Oxfordshire. A hamlet with a mixture of old and new housing, referred to by Flora Thompson as "Lark Rise". The spacious layout is at once apparent and the disorganised plan is largely a function of squatters originally settling on an area of common land.

Aerofilms Ltd.

vegetables or flowers ranges between 9 and 16 per cent of the total area' (L. D. Stamp, 1962). Very much more will be under lawns, paths and so on, so that it is probably not unlikely that gardens and open space together make up as large a proportion as two-thirds of all urban land in small settlements, compared with up to 45 per cent in cities and larger towns (Best and Coppock, 1962).

As settlements become larger, they begin to lose some of their uniformity of land use and take on expanded and different urban functions. In particular, the area under commerical use increases, sometimes forming a central core of development more in line with the generally recognised urban patterns of large towns and cities. Such differences in the composition of the urban area in small settlements, though dealt with in greater detail in Chapter 5, must be briefly mentioned here to the extent that they are illustrated clearly by Fig. 6 and Table 3. The data for the Second Land Utilisation Survey and the small settlements of East Sussex show great consistency of content, but some divergences occur with the small town map area data. These variations are to be expected as the first two data sources both refer to settlements with an average size of only 1,000 people or under. As such, they may perhaps be considered broadly to represent village settlements. In contrast, the small town map area figures refer to twelve settlements with a mean size of 7,216 persons. In these small towns, the residual category is more fully developed, taking up a quarter of the whole urban area compared with about 4 per cent in the villages. This is not only because there is a considerably expanded commercial area in small towns, but because there is also the need for a greater provision of public utility and service areas and transportation land. In addition, the industrial function of such settlements is invariably greater.

PROVISION OF LAND FOR URBAN USES

The proportionate composition of land use in small settlements provides just one side of the whole picture of land-use structure.

To both the human geographer and the economist, land is only of interest when it is directly related to people, and this is especi-

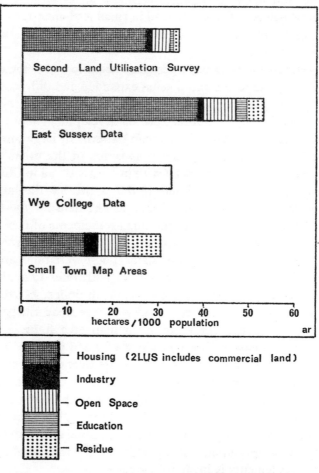

Fig. 7. The provision of urban land uses in small settlements

ally true when intensive urban land-use patterns are being studied. The concept of population density in terms of persons per hectare is the most common way by which land is related to the people

	Housing	Industry	Open space	Education	Four main uses	Residue	Total urban area
			ha/10³p				
Second Land Utilisation Survey, 1961 (260)	27·4*	1·2	4·0	0·7	33·3	1·3	34·6
East Sussex small settlement survey, 1954 (39)	38·7	1·1	7·5	2·6	49·9	3·3	53·2
Wye College small settlement survey, 1955 (213)	n.a.	n.a.	n.a.	n.a.	n.a.	n.a.	32·7
Small town map areas, 1960/61 (12)	13·9	2·7	4·6	1·8	23·0	7·6	30·6
Small town map areas, 1950 (50)	16·2	1·7	10·5	1·1	29·5	n.a.	n.a.

* Including commercial land

Table 4. The provision of urban land in small settlements

who live on it or use it; but, for planning purposes, the practice of taking a reciprocal of this measure and expressing the relationship in terms of hectares per thousand population (ha/1000p) is normally followed. This latter parameter is referred to as a provision of land or a space provision rather than a density.

As with the composition of the urban area, the data for land provisions or densities are illustrated in both tabular and diagrammatic form (Table 4 and Fig. 7). Although material from several sources is considered, the figures derived from the Second Land Utilisation Survey are of prime concern. The other sources are either deficient in the detail of land provision that they show, or else refer to special cases. The data for the sample of 213 small settlements taken in the mid-1950s, for example, only recorded the total urban area; nevertheless, the figure of 32·7 ha/1000p for the provision of all urban land as computed from this sample (Best, 1957) serves an important function in that it adds corroboration to the figure of 34·6 ha/1000p obtained from the present study.

Because of the representative basis of the sample at a national level, the data from the Second Land Utilisation Survey may, by and large, be regarded as the norm for all small settlements, against which the other data sources with their statistical deviations should be compared. These notable variations, relating to differences in the size of settlement concerned, the regional location and the economic characteristics, are dealt with in greater detail later, but their existence should be recognised at this point. It is important to understand some of the reasons for the differences in the mean provisions recorded in Table 4, and also for several of the drawbacks inherent in a consideration of the means. The case of the total urban area provision illustrates this last point very well. The mean is calculated as 34·6 ha/1000p, but attention should also be given to the distribution about this average (Fig. 8). The standard deviation of these provisions is 18·1 ha/1000p, and so at least two-thirds of such land provisions are likely to occur within the wide range 16·5–52·7 ha/1000p or, to put it another way, the coefficient of variation $\left(v = \dfrac{100s}{\bar{x}} \right)$ is 52·3 per

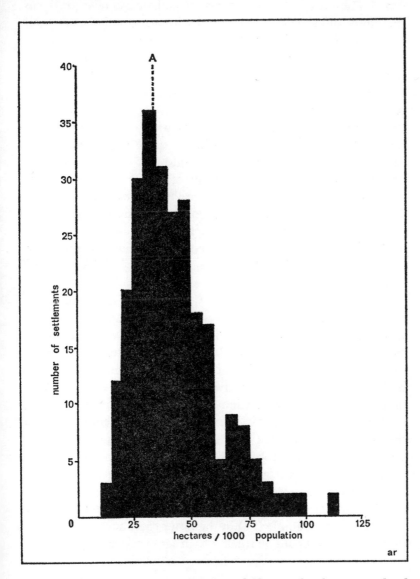

Fig. 8. The statistical distribution of the total urban area land provisions (2L.U.S.)

cent.* The use of the mean provision statistic can raise problems, therefore, and should only be used with a realisation of the considerable variation that it can sometimes hide.

Some of the rather exceptional characteristics, compared with the sample norm, which are to be seen in the data from East Sussex can be explained in terms of the small size of the sample of 39 settlements. This is particularly so, for example, with the open space provision (7·5 ha/1000p) which is made abnormally high by the large areas of open space in just one or two settlements. The size of sample could, in fact, explain other provisions which are seemingly out of line, but it may well be that land provisions in East Sussex are truly greater than average. At a later stage, regional variations in land-use structure and space provisions will be studied, and the East Sussex figures appear simply to represent the general tendency for provisions in lowland areas of England to be noticeably higher in many instances than those in upland areas.

The deviant figures for small town map areas are more readily explainable and are closely related to a major cause of variation; namely, the size of the settlements concerned. It will be explained subsequently that, as the population size of settlement increases, so does the general provision of urban land decrease. This trend is observable not only within the population range of small settlements up to 10,000 population but throughout the whole of the settlement continuum. It is, therefore, very pertinent to note that the small town map area data refer to settlements with a mean size of about 7,000 people, whereas the other data sources are concerned with a 'village-mean' of only 1,000 people or under. This size contrast is clearly reflected in the land provisions of small town map areas recorded for both 1950 and 1960/61. The small size of the sample (12) in the latter case, however, suggests that the figures should be treated with some caution, even though

---

* These measures of standard deviation and coefficient of variation apply to a normal distribution. While Fig. 8 indicates that the distribution is not completely normal and shows some skewness, the statistical measures are probably robust enough to allow their use in this case. In fact about 75 per cent of the distribution falls within the specified range.

they form a sample of supposedly typical or, rather, non-exceptional examples of this category.

Nevertheless, the figures do enable some generalisations to be made about land use in the small town, rather than the village (Table 4). Lower provisions (higher densities) in residential development are particularly evident (i.e. 14–16 ha/1000p, as compared with over 27 ha/1000p) and clearly reflect the more intense pressures on land which are present in towns compared with villages and hamlets. The industrial provision is in all cases larger than that found in smaller settlements and shows the stronger economic base present in small towns. Both this industrial figure, and the higher provision for educational land, are an indication of the greater degree of self-sufficiency found in the country town when contrasted with the village. The resident population finds an increasing amount of its service, employment and amenity requirements actually met within the settlement itself, and this provision is augmented by the need for the town to provide these facilities for the surrounding villages and hamlets as well. Moreover, above a certain size, the small town demands the provision of a specific urban infrastructure in the form of transport areas, commercial and public land, utility undertakings and the like, and this circumstance is clearly reflected in the provision of a greater residual land element which is generally of little significance in villages and hamlets.

This change towards an increased provision of the accoutrements of a truly urbanised society at the upper end of the small settlement population scale is seen again in the open space provision. The part played by the countryside as a whole in providing unrecorded and informal recreational and amenity facilities for a village population has been mentioned before, but the effect becomes progressively less important as settlements increase in size. In addition, there are strong administrative pressures on urban councils and similar bodies to provide formal areas of open space (parks, recreation grounds, etc.) in country towns which are less common at the village level. In the private sphere also, there is an increase in the supply of open space, and, out of the provision of 10·5 ha/1000p recorded for the 1950 small town map areas, 7·3 ha/1000p were in the private sector.

COMPARISONS WITH CITIES AND LARGE TOWNS

An objective, statistical account of land-use conditions in small rural settlements is of somewhat limited value by itself. The land-use structure and space provisions which are revealed only begin to take on a significant meaning when they are seen in relation to the corresponding features of larger settlements. Extensive as planning regulations are in this country, there is still a considerable degree of freedom for individual planners when it comes to making decisions on such matters as housing densities or open space provisions. Consequently, an indication of the present differences in land use between various categories of existing settlement can provide a necessary base-line in formulating acceptable and desirable standards for proposed development in the future.

The characteristics of land use in the larger settlements of England and Wales have been extensively examined in other publications (Best and Coppock, 1962; Best, 1964) and it is only necessary to outline the broad findings here. The overwhelming importance of housing as the major land-use item in the composition of the urban area of most small settlements is again emphasised from a study of Table 5, which compares and contrasts the various urban categories in England and Wales. The proportion of the urban area so used in hamlet and village-type settlements (about 80 per cent) is seen to be nearly twice that found in large settlements and county boroughs. On the other hand, there is a definite similarity between the percentage land uses in small towns of under 10,000 population and the larger types of settlement. In particular, the proportions of the total urban area under housing, industry and the residual uses shown by the small town map area data are usually of the same order as those for large towns and county boroughs. Therefore, it may be concluded that, as far as the composition of the urban area is concerned, con-

72

	Housing	Industry	Open space	Education	Four main uses	Residue
			per cent*			
Small settlements (2LUS), 1961 (260)	79·3†	3·6	11·4	2·0	96·3	3·7
Small town map areas, 1960/61 (12)	45·3	9·0	15·0	5·9	75·2	24·8
Large town map areas, 1950/51 (186)	43·5	5·3	21·5	3·0	73·3	26·7
New towns,‡ 1960/61 (12)	50·4	8·9	19·3	8·6	87·2	12·8
County boroughs, 1950/51 (79)	43·4	8·1	18·7	2·8	73·0	27·0

* Of total urban area † Including commercial land ‡ Proposed situation

Table 5. The composition of urban land in various categories of settlement

trasts are greater *within* the single overall category of small settlements than *between* the different categories of settlement which have been defined. Put another way, there exists a greater variation in urban land composition in settlements of the size range 500 to 10,000 population than in those of the range 10,000 to over 150,000. The reasons for this distinction are clearly related to the general absence of a service, commercial and industrial infrastructure in villages and hamlets – a feature which has already been noted.

This differentiation within the small settlement category is underlined again by a consideration of land provisions in the various urban groupings (Table 6 and Fig. 9). Provisions of land for most of the main uses in small towns are markedly different from those for the generality of small settlements, while, conversely, they are quite similar to those found in large towns (i.e. large town map areas). In other words, over the mean population size range from 7,000 to 30,000, land provisions do not appear to reduce very greatly, though a marked decline does occur by the time that the far more populous county boroughs are reached. Therefore a primary contrast is again indicated on the grounds of land provision characteristics between what can be called, for the sake of convenience, the village and the small town. This evidence further suggests that the present arbitrary division between the large and small settlement categories at 10,000 population is far from being satisfactory.

The deeper implications of this tendency for a progressive alteration in space standards over the whole size continuum of settlements are examined in greater detail in the following chapter. These findings are probably the first to shed light on the question of the existence or otherwise of a settlement hierarchy from the viewpoint of the man-land relationship rather than from the more traditional approach of the rank-size rule and the service functions and market areas of settlements. At this stage, however, it is worth noting from Table 6 and Fig. 9 that the overall trend is for land provisions to decrease (i.e. densities to rise) as the mean population size of settlement increases. This tendency has been called the 'hierarchy of densities' (Best,

	Average population	Housing	Industry	Open space	Education	Four main uses	Residue	Total urban area
		ha/10^3p						
Small settlements (2LUS), 1961 (260)	909	27·4*	1·2	4·0	0·7	33·3	1·3	34·6
Small town map areas, 1960/61 (12)	7,216	13·9	2·7	4·6	1·8	23·0	7·6	30·6
Large town map areas, 1950/51 (186)	31,700	12·6	2·3	6·1	1·1	22·1	7·7	29·8
New towns,† 1960/61 (12)	51,500	11·7	2·1	4·5	2·0	20·3	3·0	23·3
County boroughs, 1950/51 (79)	168,000	7·6	1·4	3·3	0·5	12·8	4·7	17·5

* Including commercial land   † Proposed situation

Table 6. The provision of urban land in various categories of settlement

1964), although it is possible that the progression is not a true, stepped hierarchy but rather a gradual adjustment over the whole

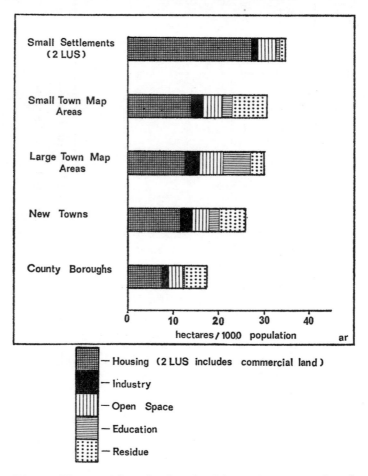

Fig. 9. The provision of urban land in various categories of settlement

range. The relationship might now more suitably be termed the density-size rule.

But whether hierarchy or continuum, the strong disparity in land use and density between village-type settlements at one end of the spectrum and county boroughs at the other is not in dispute.

76

The openness of development in villages (34·6 ha/1000p) is about twice that of the major towns and cities of England and Wales (17·5 ha/1000p), and living conditions in these small settlements, therefore, are altogether more spacious. This difference is brought out even more strongly by a consideration of residential provisions alone. In the cities and most important towns, housing provisions averaged only 7·6 ha/1000p in 1950/51 in spite of the fact that it is in these settlements that there have been extensive development and redevelopment projects, slum clearance and the like, particularly since the end of the last war. At the other extreme of the scale, villages record a mean housing provision of 27·4 ha/1000p – over three times the norm for county boroughs. Consequently, although the problem of sub-standard housing may be just as acute in some rural areas as in the big cities, small settlements nevertheless have a certain relief provided by more spacious conditions which allow for greater flexibility in redevelopment and designs for new layouts. Moreover, since it is evident that the open space allocation in county boroughs is also smaller than that in small settlements, and that the residents of these large towns and cities do not have the advantage of what may be called 'extra-settlement' recreational facilities on anything like the scale enjoyed by village populations, the contrast with regard to general living space is even more apparent.

In this way, comparisons with cities and larger towns in this country put the small settlement category properly into focus and fully endorse the impression of openness that many villages give in their land-use structure. At the outset of this discussion on the composition and provision of land in small settlements, the apparent uniformity of the land-use structure in much rural settlement was stressed as being a corollary of its predominant function of providing residential accommodation rather than a full complement of urban employment and services. Although this situation probably exists in the majority of individual small settlements, it is certainly not the case with the somewhat larger centres; and the contrasts within the small settlement category between villages and small towns have been especially emphasised. The picture as presented is still essentially a very generalised one, however. Accordingly, the next three chapters attempt to demonstrate some of the more detailed aspects of the subject by elaborating on, and attempting to rationalise, the many variations in land use existing within the whole category of small settlements.

5 · Variations in Land Use and Density of Development

In attempting to present a detailed model of land use in small settlements to augment and amplify the rather generalised outline already given, there are two main groups of problems which must again be mentioned. First, there is the great variety of physical, economic and social constraints that influence land-use patterns, and, second, there is the frequently unquantifiable nature of the many variables which are involved. As so much of English rural settlement is the product of a long and varied history, often stretching back over more than a thousand years, both these sets of problems are to be expected.

In constructing a model, it would not be too difficult to simplify the complications of multi-causality by a judicious choice of likely variables, albeit chosen on a rather subjective basis. Therefore, a set of physical controls could be postulated in terms of, say, altitude or the degree of relief dissection, and to these items could be added factors involving the local economy of the region, the pattern of land holding and other tenurial arrangements, and perhaps even a consideration of the ethnic idiosyncrasies which so intrigued scholars in the nineteenth century. All these items, and many more, are eminently reasonable as explanatory variables; but there still remains the major analytical problem that so many of them cannot really be measured. Factors such as tenurial arrangements are essentially of a non-quantifiable nature, while even those economic variables which are normally subject to precise measurement are not so in this case, if only because the relevant statistics for earlier historical periods do not exist.

Consequently, the impossibility of producing a strongly-based quantitative model is obvious. The alternatives would seem to be two-fold. First, it might be possible to analyse the processes of small settlement growth in this country and from these observations construct a normative model to explain past growth and development. The use of simulation procedures could well be of use in this context. In effect, such a method would consider the pattern of decision-making on the part of the individuals forming the population of the settlements concerned and would link these decisions to the resulting land patterns. The method would, in fact, be primarily concerned with the behavioural characteristics of people. In contrast, the other alternative is simply to study the existing land patterns, ignoring at the first stage the actual decision processes behind them, and then provide a model concerned with the characteristics of the settlements alone. In so doing, the analysis becomes largely a descriptive outline of the variations in the characteristics of small settlements.

This second approach is the method used here. While it is certainly less ambitious than that suggested for studying human decision-making, it has the advantage that it is better suited to the present data. Moreover, if the results of this work are to be of any interest to planners who are concerned initially with the landscape as it now exists, then it is better if the investigation is put in terms that are more immediately applicable. A behavioural model has immense possibilities for explaining human action, environmental perception and the like, but what is really needed first of all is a more mundane analysis of facts as they exist. Accordingly, an attempt has been made here to provide a detailed analysis and evaluation of the variation which occurs within the broad picture already presented of land use in small settlements.

THE METHODOLOGY OF SIZE ANALYSIS

The first part of this analysis has been to examine the variations that exist in both the composition of the urban area and in the densities of development as a progression is made from the small-

III. Nun Monkton,
Yorkshire. A classic
example of a green
village, complete with
pond and a genuine
maypole. The wide
expanse of the green
with its surrounding
buildings has resulted
in space provisions
which are particularly
open.

Aerofilms Ltd.

IV. Pegswood, North-
umberland. A mining
village with character-
istic 19th century
housing of high density
built on a rigid pattern
close to the pithead.
The outskirts of the
settlement (left back-
ground) have an area
of recent estate de-
velopment at a much
lower density.

Aerofilms Ltd.

est hamlet to the town of 10,000 people at the other end of the small settlement scale. In effect, this study is of the changes which occur over the size continuum, on the hypothesis that they will probably take the form of increasing densities and a larger proportion of non-residential land uses as progress is made towards more populous and 'urban' forms of settlement. Qualitative perception apart, there is considerable evidence that this is indeed the case, although there has been little attempt to express it in specific, quantitative terms. One of the present authors previously discussed this tendency as it appeared from his original urban data (Best, 1957), and the progression is very apparent as well in grouped data for the four main urban uses derived from analyses of development plans and recorded in Table 7 (Ministry of Housing and Local Government, 1958). Such a trend was also

Population of towns		Existing provision*	Proposed provision
		ha/10³p	ha/10³p
Over 500,000	(5)	11·5	15·6
200–500,000	(12)	12·1	16·4
100–200,000	(43)	14·7	19·0
50–100,000	(65)	18·9	23·2
20–50,000	(92)	21·6	25·7
10–20,000	(48)	25·0	28·7
Under 10,000	(50)	29·5	33·3

Size of town sample in each population category indicated in brackets
* About 1950

Table 7. Provisions of land for the four main urban uses in county boroughs and town map areas analysed by size of town

referred to in the previous chapter when comparisons were made between the statistics for mainly hamlets and villages obtained from the Second Land Utilisation Survey and the data for small towns and larger urban centres provided by development plans.

The collection of data from the Second Land Utilisation Survey has now made a new analysis possible because the settlements involved are a representative statistical sample which fall within the population range from 0 up to 10,000 (but excluding isolated dwellings) with no section of the continuum being unrepresented. In addition, some use is also made of the data collected for small settlements in East Sussex, even though there are problems with these figures resulting from the relatively small size of the total sample. The same problem of sample size is even more serious in the case of the statistics for the small town map areas, while the earlier data collected at Wye College have been rejected at this stage of the analysis because of the somewhat arbitrary nature of the sample and because the information refers only to the total urban area and not to the constituent uses.

The present analysis largely depends, therefore, on the use of the main data source for this study, the Second Land Utilisation Survey, and the investigation has been carried out at two levels. In the first place, the ungrouped data for all 260 small settlements have been considered, while at a later stage these settlements are arranged in size groupings and the analysis is repeated for the groups. As will become clear, this last procedure is useful because it removes much of the variation caused by factors other than the size of the settlement and therefore enables the general trend along the continuum to be studied. Conversely, of course, this grouping procedure necessarily hides the within-group variation, and so the analysis of the ungrouped data is also required to put the trends observed into their true perspective. Unfortunately, however, it will be recalled that the 260 small settlements are themselves an aggregation of 488 still smaller villages and hamlets which cannot be analysed separately because of the unavailability of detailed population data below the parish level. Although this circumstance probably has little importance when the composition of the urban area is being considered, its effect is likely to be rather more significant when an analysis of the relationship of density to settlement-size is undertaken. In the subsequent analysis, this qualification should be borne in mind, for, in effect, the data have been grouped initially to some small extent. This procedure is not entirely satisfactory, but is unavoidable in the present state of data deficiencies if any attempt at analysis is to be made at all.

The 39 small settlements comprising the East Sussex data were chosen by statistical procedure whereby all the small settlements in the county were ranked in relation to the logarithm of their population size, the ranking obtained being divided into quintiles. Sampling was then carried out within the strata. As a result, the sampling procedure itself provides the groupings for the size analysis, with the results given in Table 8.

Group	Class interval	Mean population size of group	Number in group
1	19–66	47	5
2	67–211	130	8
3	212–674	357	10
4	675–2,151	1,146	10
5	2,152–8,078	4,126	6

Table 8. East Sussex small settlements by size groupings

A major drawback with this method is that it tends to under-represent the large number of smaller settlements at the bottom end of the size continuum by taking no account of the distribution of settlement sizes noted in Chapter 3 (Fig. 5). Because the method of quintile division was an integral part of the sampling process rather than a specific means of size-analysis, it was impossible to regroup the East Sussex data without destroying the statistical validity of the entire sample. With the Second Land Utilisation Survey, however, it was possible to group the settlements by another method which is more suited to present purposes. To this end, the 260 small settlements concerned were plotted on a scatter diagram. The required groupings were then organised to take account of obvious breaks in the array and the corresponding clusters. By this means, eight groups of settlements were derived which not only gave sufficiently large group sizes but also allowed true representation of the large number of small settlements at the lower end of the scale. The results of this procedure are given in Table 9.

Before turning to the analysis itself, one other point of methodology should be mentioned. For analytical purposes, an index of settlement size must be determined against which land provision, or density, may be compared. The population contained within a settlement is the most common index to be employed rather than the total area of a settlement, partly because of the greater availability of population statistics. As this measure also facilitates comparisons between various settlement studies and has other practical advantages, it is the index which has been chosen here as well.

Group	Class interval	Mean population size of group	Number in group
1	0–199	110	67
2	200–399	293	64
3	400–599	475	30
4	600–799	709	18
5	800–1,199	983	24
6	1,200–1,999	1,556	25
7	2,000–3,999	2,525	18
8	4,000–10,000	5,375	14

Table 9. Second Land Utilisation Survey:
small settlements by size groupings

The relationship between population and land area is a relatively close one, although recent work suggests that policies of slum clearance, rehousing at lower densities and infilling have sometimes tended to blur the connection in the case of large urban areas (Best and Champion, 1970). Even though this study attempts to review the variations which exist in the relationship by reason of changes in size, location and economic structure, there remains, nevertheless, a link between the two factors. Taking the grouped data, as explained above, and plotting the mean population total against the land area, the exact nature of the relationship is made clear (Fig. 10). For each of the three most important land uses in small settlements – housing and commercial land, open space and the total urban area – the relationships were plotted and then a least-squares regression was performed. This showed that a strong linear relationship did in fact exist between the two factors at this generalised level, as indicated by the high correlation coefficients obtained:

$$\text{Total urban area/population} = 0\cdot99890$$
$$\text{Residential and commercial area/population} = 0\cdot99583$$
$$\text{Open space area/population} = 0\cdot99853$$

(All significant at $P = 0\cdot001$)

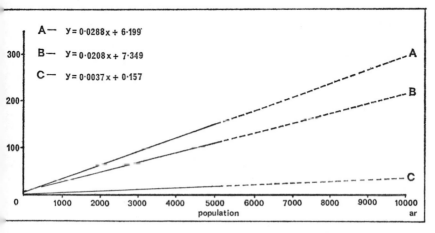

Fig. 10. The relationship between the population size of small settlements (2L.U.S.) and the area of urban land uses: A=total urban area; B=residential (and commercial) area; C=open space area

Mathematical expressions can be obtained for the three relationships. These may be plotted as in Fig. 10, and present a clearer picture of the absolute change in land area over the population range 0–10,000. Therefore, it is possible to gain a more accurate idea of the average size of the individual units making up the sample. Just as the population range rises from 0 to 10,000 people, so is it clear that the upper extreme of the areal range might reach about 300 ha or more for the largest small settlements.

85

SIZE VARIATIONS IN URBAN AREA COMPOSITION

Data on the composition of the urban area are complicated to assess *en masse*, not only because of the multiplicity of statistics but also because the percentage figures are all related to a common base and are therefore liable to distortion if only one use is particularly variable. This distortion is especially noticeable in relation to the residual category which often influences the proportions recorded for the other uses. Accordingly, variations in land-use composition are best studied in terms of collective mean figures, and so the use of the grouped size data is called for in this instance.

Group	Mean popula- tion size	Housing*	Indus- try	Open space	Educa- tion	Four main uses	Residue
				per cent†			
1	110	81·4	2·1	11·4	1·6	96·5	3·5
2	293	83·3	1·0	10·6	1·2	96·1	3·9
3	475	84·4	1·3	10·3	1·0	97·0	3·0
4	709	81·4	1·4	10·5	1·0	94·3	5·7
5	983	82·5	2·4	11·1	0·9	96·9	3·1
6	1,556	82·7	2·8	10·0	1·2	96·7	3·3
7	2,525	79·0	1·9	12·0	3·4	96·3	3·7
8	5,375	72·6	7·8	12·9	2·9	96·2	3·8
Overall means	909	79·3	3·6	11·4	2·0	96·3	3·7

* Including commercial land   † Of total urban area

Table 10. Second Land Utilisation Survey: variations in the composition of the total urban area of small settlements of different size

The variations in the composition of the total urban area as obtained from the main data source, the Second Land Utilisation Survey, are recorded in Table 10 in relation to the eight size groupings mentioned previously. Table 11 deals with a similar breakdown of the data for East Sussex. In this latter table, the problems associated with small sub-sample numbers are particularly clear in Group 3, where an exceptional area of public open space in two of the ten settlements recorded for that group tends to overweight the category in relation to the other uses.

Group	Mean population size	Housing	Indus- try	Open space	Educa- tion	Four main uses	Residue
				per cent*			
1	47	87·6	–	–	–	87·6	12·4
2	130	87·9	3·9	0·6	1·9	94·3	5·7
3	357	70·5	2·0	19·7	0·7	92·9	7·1
4	1,146	80·2	3·2	7·3	2·6	93·3	6·7
5	4,126	69·1	1·7	16·7	6·8	94·3	5·7
Overall means	1,053	72·7	2·1	14·1	4·9	93·8	6·2

* Of total urban area

Table 11. East Sussex small settlements: variations in the composition of the total urban area of small settlements of different size

This last difficulty apart, both tables clearly re-emphasise the predominant importance of housing in small settlement land use – about 80 per cent of the total area of hamlets, villages and very small towns being used for residential purposes. Within the population size range 4,000–5,000 the proportion falls towards 70 per cent, and this situation is underlined when it is remembered that, from small town map area data, it was estimated that only about 45 per cent of the total urban area was under residential uses. Therefore, the trend indicated is one of a declining proportional area under housing as settlements become larger, with 80 per cent or more of the urban area under this use in the smallest villages and hamlets but only about 45 per cent occupied in this way by the time small towns of 7,000 people are reached.

Since the available figures for larger towns and county boroughs suggest that the proportion of land under housing is still about 43 per cent (Table 5), the decline probably tends to level off after this threshold.

Contrasts in Table 10, and especially between Groups 1–7 and the much more populous Group 8, are again clear with respect to industrial land, except that the tendency is in the reverse direction from that of housing. Probably up to a settlement size of 4–5,000 people, industry generally remains relatively unimportant at around 1–3 per cent of the total area, whereas, above 5,000 population, the area is of the order of 8–9 per cent.

Trends in the proportional importance of open space and land used for educational purposes are less easily ascertained from the data. It is likely that there is a slight increase in the proportion of land under both uses as settlement size increases, and particularly so by the time the population has reached the size of a small town. However, there is some evidence that, in larger cities and towns of over 30,000 population, the slightly upward trend in provision for both uses begins to reverse itself (Best and Coppock, 1962).

These two uses of open space and education, when considered together with housing and industry, comprise the four main urban uses. In aggregate, these uses show a marked consistency in land percentage up to the tentatively suggested threshold limit at least. Only when settlements become truly urban, in both population size and functional character, do the remaining residual uses begin to assume a significantly increased proportion of the total urban area. The increased importance of this residual element is clearly seen from the data for the twelve ungrouped small town map areas shown in Table 12, where the residual uses account for nearly a quarter of the total urban area. However, the very restricted size of this sample of small towns inevitably means that the trends in land composition noted for the two other data sources are not evident in this third case. Clearly, while such tendencies undoubtedly exist, they are not apparent by taking individual examples and very small samples in which special characteristics intrude too blatantly. Therefore, a major problem in the analysis of rural settlement is again highlighted; namely, the contrasting individuality of the units involved which makes the recognition of overall tendencies extremely difficult. Only by the amalgamation of a large number of such units into groups is it possible to overcome the effects of the individual variations and expose the prevalent trends.

Small town map areas	Popula-tion	Hous-ing	Indus-try	Open space	Educa-tion	Four main uses	Residue
			per cent*				
Dolgellau	2,500	47·0	10·1	13·1	6·6	76·8	23·2
Thornbury	3,198	47·0	12·6	20·0	1·5	81·1	18·9
Whaley Bridge	5,210	31·3	9·8	15·4	2·6	59·1	40·9
Alnwick	7,280	56·0	12·1	11·0	6·1	85·2	14·8
Whitworth	7,300	39·6	1·7	14·1	22·1	77·5	22·5
Wombourn	8,000	64·2	7·7	3·6	5·3	80·8	19·2
Biggleswade	8,070	32·4	11·2	17·1	1·6	62·3	37·7
New Mills	8,185	38·1	9·3	14·4	2·1	63·9	36·1
Milnrow	8,400	30·1	1·5	20·1	24·9	76·6	23·4
Clay Cross	9,250	54·0	3·4	27·9	8·5	93·8	6·2
Witney	9,400	50·9	12·1	18·3	6·6	87·9	12·1
Northallerton	9,800	47·7	5·4	8·8	6·1	68·0	32·0
Overall means	7,216	45·3	9·0	15·0	5·9	75·2	24·8

* Of total urban area

Table 12. Small town map areas: variations in the composition of the total urban area of small settlements of different size

THE DENSITY-SIZE RULE

The need for the amalgamation of settlement units to point out the important motifs behind the land-use structure is again relevant when differences in the intensity of urban land use are considered. However, the changes here over the size range 0–10,000 population are perhaps rather more clear-cut than in the case of the figures for proportional composition. Providing that a sufficiently large number of settlements is included in the sample, they can be studied in an ungrouped form, even though the other variables involved apart from population size complicate the pattern to some extent.

In fact, it was through a study of ungrouped data that the first concepts on the relationship between size of settlement and the densities at which people live were suggested (Best, 1957). The density contrasts between, for example, villages and small towns on the one hand and county boroughs on the other were obvious enough and suggested that, as population size of settlement increased, the density tightened up as well (Table 7). This hypothesis naturally led to the idea that there might exist an important trend within the single but wide category of small settlements; between, that is, hamlets at the one extreme and small towns at the other. Some indications that this situation existed were seen in Chapter 4 where it appeared that contrasts in land provision were probably greater between, for example, hamlets and small towns than between small towns and larger towns and cities.

The present research at last enables a more precise appraisal of these contrasts and trends. The data have been analysed both in the ungrouped state and then in the size groupings which were discussed previously. As will be seen, whereas the first type of analysis presents a more correct picture of the true influence of the size factor with regard to land provisions, the second analysis of the grouped data has the effect of removing many of the idiosyncrasies and so exposing the general trend more distinctly. Of the variables which might help in an explanation of land patterns and provisions in small settlements, the size of the population is probably the only one which is easily and immediately quantifiable. Most others, for reasons that have already been explained, are either unquantifiable or else irrelevant by reason of time differences. Had more variables been suitably quantifiable, then the analysis could have been more comprehensive and might well have used such techniques as factor analysis or multiple regression. As it was, the one method which was immediately acceptable was least-squares regression involving the only variable which could be quantified – population size.

The initial inspection of the figures for land provision from the Second Land Utilisation Survey data suggested that, if a relationship between population size of settlement and total urban land provision truly existed, then it was unlikely to be of a simple linear form. Accordingly, use was made of a regression programme (Genstep 4) which, although meant for multiple regression involving several variables, could also be used for present purposes in order to find the nature of the relationship being studied. Various transformations of both population size and total urban area provision were tested and the best-fit model was obtained. In the event, this model involved a log-transformation of both variables and was of the form:

$$\log y = 1{\cdot}9986 - 0{\cdot}1522 \log x \ldots\ldots\ldots(1)$$
$$\text{where } y = \text{total land provision (ha/1000p)}$$
$$\text{and } x = \text{population of settlement}$$
$$Sb = 0{\cdot}0193$$

In words rather than figures, the general relationship can be stated in the following way: as the population size of settlement increases the land provision falls exponentially (i.e. the density of development rises).

Although this function, which may be called the density-size rule, best describes the relationship between population size and total urban land provision for the 260 small settlements of the sample, the presence of so many other variables inevitably gives a low level of explanation overall. In fact, the correlation coefficient (significant at $P = 0{\cdot}001$) is $-0{\cdot}4405$, i.e. $r^2 = 0{\cdot}1940$. In other words, no more than 19·4 per cent of the variation in the provision of urban land can be 'explained' with reference to the population size of the settlement. Quite obviously considerable care would be needed in using the results of this analysis in any predictive capacity. Nevertheless, it should be remembered that the prime motive behind the investigation was not in fact predictive, as might be the case with some types of demand analysis, but was essentially descriptive of the nature of land use in small settlements. Some progress has clearly been made in this respect in that an important element in small settlement land use has been isolated, its statistical significance proved, and an indication given of 'average' land-use conditions for particular settlement sizes.

The density-size rule specified above is shown in a diagrammatic form in Fig. 11. The general trend towards a decreasing provision of urban land as the population size of a settlement increases is immediately apparent and is made more obvious by the presence of the best-fit curve. The scatter of points about this line is indicative, of course, of the rather low level of explanation, but this distribution is useful in so far as it enables a further stage in the analysis to be completed. The consideration of the characteristics of the residuals from the best-fit curve helps to throw further light on the rationale behind the land pattern, and so the model described above will be used in this way in subsequent chapters.

It is obviously impractical to attempt a regression of this type on the data for the 12 small town map areas simply because the variation among the small number of settlements in the sample would completely disturb any general trend. In the case of the East Sussex small settlement data, however, the sample size does warrant similar treatment. Again, a least-squares regression was performed on the transformed variables of population size and total urban land provision, and the results obtained were similar to those for the Second Land Utilisation Survey data (Fig. 12). This time a log-transformation of the population variable alone provided the best-fit solution with a correlation coefficient of -0.3866 (significant at $P = 0.02$) and an r^2 of 0.1494. In this instance the mathematical function obtained was:

$$y = 105.6932 - 17.6693 \log x \ldots \ldots (2)$$
$$Sb = 6.7489$$

where x and y have the same meaning as in equation (1).

Despite the problems of multi-causality, therefore, it has been possible to trace the behaviour of land provisions over the relevant size range. The log-log relationship which gives the best

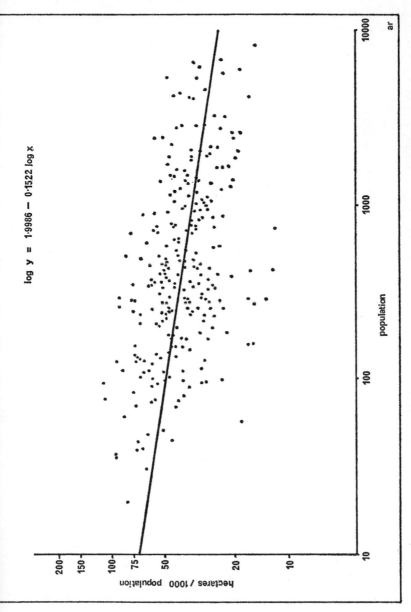

Fig. 11. Second Land Utilisation Survey: the relationship between the provision of land for the total urban area of small settlements and the population size

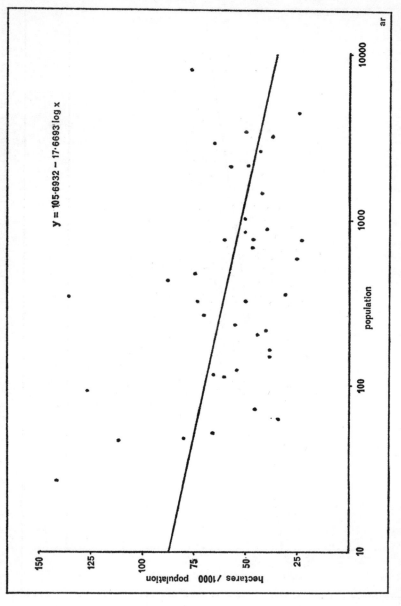

$y = 105.6932 - 17.6693 \log x$

Fig. 12. East Sussex small settlements: the relationship between the provision of land for the total urban

explanation of the density-size rule provides a more accurate description of this behaviour than merely saying that land provisions tend to decrease as population size increases. Nevertheless, it is possible to remove the influence of some of the extraneous factors which cause within-sample variations by grouping the data as described previously. Providing it is remembered that the relationship between population size and land provision is thereby merely highlighted, and by so doing its seeming importance as an explanatory variable is necessarily exaggerated to some extent, then such a process need not be misleading. The true *extent* of the relationship has been explained by the analysis of ungrouped data; its *nature* can best be understood by the examination of grouped material.

Group	Mean population size	Housing*	Industry	Open space	Education	Four main uses	Residue	Total urban area
				ha/10³p				
1	110	40·8	1·1	5·7	0·8	48·4	1·7	50·1
2	293	36·0	0·4	4·6	0·5	41·5	1·7	43·2
3	475	35·6	0·5	4·4	0·4	40·9	1·3	42·2
4	709	35·1	0·5	4·5	0·5	40·6	2·5	43·1
5	983	29·9	0·9	4·0	0·3	35·1	1·1	36·2
6	1,556	28·0	0·9	3·4	0·4	32·7	1·1	33·8
7	2,525	24·9	0·6	3·7	1·1	30·3	1·2	31·5
8	5,375	21·6	2·3	3·8	1·0	28·7	1·1	29·8
Overall means	909	27·4	1·2	4·0	0·7	33·3	1·3	34·6

* Including commercial land

Table 13. Second Land Utilisation Survey: variations in the provision of urban land uses in small settlements of different size

The main group provisions for the five constituent land uses of the total urban area were calculated for both the Second Land Utilisation Survey and the East Sussex data, and the results are presented in Tables 13 and 14. The problems associated with the small sample size of some of the groups for East Sussex appear again and are seen in the high open space provisions for Groups

3 and 5, which naturally affect the composite totals. Although allowance can be made for this bias, and the underlying trends are then clear, it is more convenient to consider only the Second Land Utilisation Survey data in detail.

Group	Mean population size	Housing	Industry	Open space	Education	Four main uses	Residue	Total urban area
				ha/10³p				
1	47	68·6	–	–	–	68·6	9·8	78·4
2	130	48·7	2·2	0·3	1·1	52·3	3·1	55·4
3	357	45·0	1·3	12·5	0·4	59·2	4·6	63·8
4	1,146	38·6	1·5	3·5	1·3	44·9	3·2	48·1
5	4,126	37·2	0·9	8·9	3·6	50·6	3·1	53·7
Overall means	1,053	38·7	1·1	7·5	2·6	49·9	3·3	53·2

Table 14. East Sussex small settlements: variations in the provision of urban land uses in small settlements of different size

The trend of a decreasing provision of land as settlement size increases is immediately evident from a study of both sets of figures, particularly with regard to the individual uses of housing and open space and the composite four main uses and total urban area. Thus, residential provisions fall from over 40 ha/1000p for a hamlet-sized settlement to about 30–35 ha/1000p by the time a settlement of village size is reached (c. 750 persons). Thereafter, although the decline continues, it is at a reduced rate relative to the increase in population size. The change in the open space element is less dramatic, but basically follows the same pattern of high provision in the smallest settlements (about 6 ha/1000p), falling to a lower provision in larger-sized settlements. Intensities of use as far as industry and education are concerned are less clear-cut, though with settlements of a more urban nature these uses are naturally of greater importance and the provision of necessary facilities is therefore somewhat larger than in lower-rank settlements.

The overall trends in land provision are best seen by a consideration of the data for housing and the total urban area. The disadvantage of dealing with a single mean figure (34·6 ha/1000p) is now apparent, as the computed range over which the total urban land provisions spread is of the order of 20 ha/1000p for

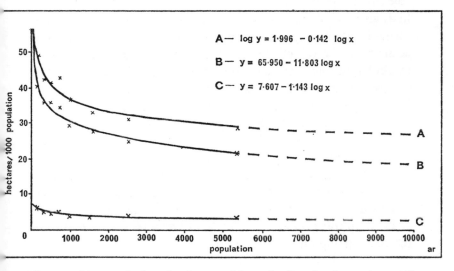

$$A— \log y = 1·996 - 0·142 \log x$$

$$B— y = 65·950 - 11·803 \log x$$

$$C— y = 7·607 - 1·143 \log x$$

Fig. 13. Size variations in the provision of urban land uses in small settlements (2L.U.S.): A=total urban area; B=residential (and commercial) area; C=open space area

the grouped data alone and is, of course, much larger when individual settlements are considered. As was the case with the ungrouped data, a diagrammatic representation of these figures makes the situation clear. The three most important quantities in an assessment of small settlement land use are the total urban area and the areas under housing and open space. The other categories are either composite, as with the four main uses, or else are less extensive and less prone to general regularities. Further analysis along these lines is particularly relevant since land under both housing and open space plays an all-important part in the living space available to the population. If the grouped data means for these three items are plotted against the mean population size, as in Fig. 13, the relationship broadly suggested by the earlier analysis of the ungrouped data is again emphasised.

Once more, least-squares regression was used to find both the quantitative nature of the relationships and also the best-fit curves which would simplify the observed pattern, or the density-size rule. In all three cases, the correlation coefficients indicated a high level of explanation with regard to the most suitable transformation (Table 15), and so the best-fit curves can be taken as an accurate portrayal of the total distribution (Fig. 13), with a reminder of the fact that the grouping of the data naturally exaggerates the trend. On each occasion, there occurs a sharp fall in the respective provision figures over the first part of the size range. The decline in the provision of open space is the least abrupt, but with the total urban area and residential/commercial provisions there is a particularly distinctive pattern. By the time a population size of about 2,000 is reached (i.e. a large village or very small town), the main part of the decline in provision has taken place, although the diminution still continues slowly thereafter. With this process in mind, it will now be useful to examine the relationship on a wider front.

Urban land category	Mathematical function	Correlation coefficient	Sb
Total urban area provision	$\log y = 1 \cdot 996 - 0 \cdot 142 \log x$	$-0 \cdot 96815^{\star}$	$0 \cdot 013$
Residential/commercial provision	$y = 65 \cdot 950 - 11 \cdot 803 \log x$	$-0 \cdot 97779^{\star}$	$0 \cdot 895$
Open space provision	$y = 7 \cdot 607 - 1 \cdot 143 \log x$	$-0 \cdot 85776\dagger$	$0 \cdot 242$

where y = land provision (ha/1000p)
and x = population of settlement
$\star$ = significant at $P = 0 \cdot 001$
$\dagger$ = significant at $P = 0 \cdot 01$

Table 15. Functions of variation in urban land-use provision in small settlements

DENSITY COMPARISONS WITH LARGER SETTLEMENTS

The major purpose of this study is an analysis of land use in small settlements, not a consideration of the whole settlement hierarchy. Nevertheless, the behaviour of one element in this set may have important implications for settlements of a higher order. Put more directly, it must be asked whether the relationships sketched out in Fig. 13 have a relevance for large towns and cities as well as for small settlements.

	Large settlements (Mean size = c. 43,000)		County boroughs (Mean size = c. 165,000)	
	A	B	A	B
	ha/10³p			
Total urban area provision	29·5	21·8	17·5	18·0
Residential/commercial provision	12·8	11·3	7·6	4·4
Open space provision	6·4	2·3	3·3	1·7

A = calculated provision (Best and Coppock, 1962)
B = estimated provision from Second Land Utilisation Survey data

Table 16. Actual and projected land-use provisions:
a comparison of development plan data and Second Land
Utilisation Survey projections

The availability of data for larger settlements from development plans (Best, 1962) enables something of a cross-check to be performed on the functions obtained for small settlements. Clearly, if the progression indicated by Fig. 13 holds true over the whole settlement hierarchy, then the substitution of the respective population sizes in the equations should yield results which are at least partially comparable with those derived from development plan data. This substitution has been carried out, and the results are recorded in Table 16. On the whole, it is seen that the use of the calculated functions tends to underestimate the land provisions in larger towns and cities, although the

99

correspondence is close in the case of the total urban area provision for county boroughs and the residential provision for large settlements.

It would seem that the discrepancies noted can be partly explained by the fact that the rate of decline in land provisions levels out to a greater extent than the curves relating to small settlements would indicate by themselves. The reasoning behind this point is clear enough. At one end of the scale, where settlements are very small and land provisions very high, there is theoretically no practical upper limit to the looseness of development until separate, individual dwellings are reached. But as settlements get larger and land provisions fall, there must come a point at which social factors, and the associated biological and medical problems resulting from overcrowding, conspire to prevent any further decrease in space standards, unless enormous high-rise structures are built. Of perhaps even more significance, notable changes in residual provisions probably have a marked effect in the middle ranges of the density-size rule curve.

It is demonstrably unrealistic, therefore, to apply a rule obtained over one small section of the settlement hierarchy right across the whole sequence in a very precise way. Indeed, if the logic of the situation is taken to absurd lengths, it follows that land provisions will eventually decline towards zero, although the settlements concerned would have a population beyond the bounds of reason. Nevertheless, the substitution exercise has not been wasted, for it suggests that the density-size rule relationship, after the initial steepness at the minor end of the scale, does progress, though not necessarily at a constant rate, towards what may be called a terminal figure in the case of the largest cities.

Although the density-size rule has not previously been applied to the settlement pattern of England and Wales, a number of associated density-distance relationships, which have generally been variations upon the negative exponential function of Clark (1951), have been used. However, Bartholomew (1955) and Clawson, Held and Stoddard (1960) have in fact studied the link between density and population size for certain American cities, with results that closely follow the pattern noted previously in this chapter. But some time before this work was done, Bogue (1949) had also studied the population characteristics around 67 American cities and had shown that densities declined with distance from the central city in a regular, logarithmic fashion. Moreover, his research suggested that the rate of decline varied with the size of the central city, and so effectively anticipated the later work on this subject. Discussions on the behaviour of population densities at increasing distances from a central city have similarly been used by Vining (1955) in his arguments favouring a continuum of settlement sizes rather than a more rigid, Christaller-type, hierarchy. Vining also postulates a general pattern of decreasing densities with increasing distance from a metropolis and therefore, by implication, with decreasing size of settlement.

There is, then, substantial evidence that the density-size rule outlined in this chapter has a general validity outside the restricted context of small settlements in England and Wales. Accordingly, there is some justification for considering it together with Zipf's rank-size rule (1949) and Clark's negative exponential function as another example of what Johnson (1967) has termed 'gradient analysis' in settlement geography.

It is possible that this progression is simply another aspect of the operation of the urban land market (W. Alonso, 1960 and 1964). Just as urban population densities have been observed to decline exponentially away from the city centre (C. Clark, 1951; B. J. L. Berry, J. W. Simmons and R. J. Tennant, 1963), so may the same effect be seen in small settlement land use. In hamlets and small villages land is ample and relatively cheap, so it tends to be used more extensively and, in the past, even extravagantly. But as the population grows, the demand for land increases and the substitution of other inputs for land takes place. As a result, these other inputs will be reflected in higher densities and tighter development patterns which will help to lighten the burden of land rents and values which have been forced up by the increased demand.

In conclusion, it should be emphasised that the curve associated with the density-size rule, like that of Clark's density-distance rule, will alter its shape and position over time. This is indicated, for example, by the grouped data for the four main urban uses derived from development plans and recorded in Table 7. Here it is seen that the planning proposals for each size category of settlement show a fairly consistent increase in land provision of some 4 ha/1000p compared with the existing situation. However, these figures record only the *intentions* of planners, not the actual results achieved. Even so, it is clear from the work of Bruce (1967) that densities have been loosening out in many urban areas since about 1950.

There is other evidence, nevertheless, which suggests that an opening out of densities in some areas may be paralleled by a tightening up in others. At a regional level, such a situation is particularly implied by a study of recent county changes in urban growth (Best and Champion, 1970), while at the local level it is to be seen in the process of infilling and in the construction of new, less open, development on the fringes of small settlements (see Chapter 8). Both these trends contribute to the idea of a so-called 'pivotal' density or provision (Clark, 1967), towards which there is a certain convergence of space standards with higher density areas losing population and lower density areas gaining it. For England and Wales, the pivotal density for the total urban area of a settlement has been put at around 30–35 ha/1000p (Best, 1968b and 1972). If this concept has validity, it suggests that the slope of the density-size rule curve may be tending, over time, towards an almost horizontal position. In actual fact, of course, such an extreme circumstance is never likely to be attained, although it is entirely conceivable that a much flatter curve, reflecting an evening out of densities, might well be the result of present trends. The significance of this process for the character of English rural settlement will be considered in a subsequent chapter.

6 · Regional Differences in Land Use

So far, the land-use structure of small settlements has been discussed very largely from an overall, national viewpoint, with little
reference to any regional variations in land provision or density
which reflect differences in both the physical and cultural environments. Yet the regional approach has had a long, though
somewhat unsettled, history in geographical investigation, and it
is not surprising, therefore, that most of the work which has
formerly occupied workers in the field of rural settlement studies
has had a pronounced regional bias.

Another important characteristic of previous work on the subject is that it has very often been the prerogative of the historical
geographer. As a result, many of the concepts put forward to
explain observed patterns have concentrated on two main
aspects: the importance of cultural dissemination associated with
the migration of population groups; and the dominance of the
natural environment in influencing the site and type of settlement
chosen by particular peoples. In this way, it has become custom-
ary to make a fundamental distinction between nucleation and
dispersion in settlement form at a regional level and to explain
both forms with reference either to so-called physical or environmental factors or else to the influence of cultural elements.

Environmental influences are generally taken to refer to the
complex of relief, slope, aspect, soils, climate, hydrology and
vegetation which are considered to have been of prime importance in the original siting of a settlement and to have subsequently influenced its pattern and progress of growth. The
presence or otherwise of groundwater, for example, has provided
a particularly valuable factor for geographers in the explanation

of settlement patterns. Therefore, scarcity of water supply, as in limestone areas, supposedly favours the nucleation of population around the few water sources available, while abundant water supply leads to dispersed settlement forms or, at the extreme, discourages settlement almost entirely when the land becomes marshy. On a more local scale, 'dry-point' and 'wet-point' sites have traditionally been called upon to explain the initial location of individual settlements (e.g. S. H. Beaver, 1943). Such physical explanations are perhaps specially appropriate in a country like Britain where strong environmental contrasts exist over comparatively short distances.

The cultural reasons put forward to explain settlement conformation and siting have been largely related to the economies of the peoples first settling the areas in question. Such explanations were particularly popular at the end of the nineteenth century and are especially associated with the name of August Meitzen (1895). In their simplest outline, these theories attempted to relate the form of settlement to the husbandry patterns of specific ethnic groups. In the British context, therefore, a distinction has been drawn between the dispersed settlement patterns, characteristic of Celtic agrarian and pastoral practices on individual farms, and the nucleated villages associated with the agriculture of the Anglo-Saxons and Normans and the communal organisation of the open-field system (for a recent example, see P. Allerston, 1970).

While C. T. Smith (in R. J. Chorley and P. Haggett, 1965) is certainly correct when he contends that, since the last war, work along these lines has been 'on a more local and often on a more intensive scale than the pioneer works of early writers', the fact remains that the basic method of approach has changed little from the dual attitude described above. Certainly the day is long past when scholars produced their varying brands of environmental and cultural determinism to explain the characteristics of rural settlement; but there often remains, nevertheless, a strong subjective element in such work. Again, while the change to a more local and intensive viewpoint is often to be welcomed in the interests of academic rigour, there is a distinct danger that, in this way, researchers will merely expend their energies exploring some intellectual cul-de-sac while ignoring the broader picture which is of a more widespread application. Although extreme generalisations like those of the Meitzen school are as well forgotten, it is perhaps doubtful whether there is much value in replacing them by a series of largely unrelated myopic studies which contribute little to an overall understanding.

Of course, this is not to say that past work concerning regional characteristics of rural settlement has been entirely profitless. It is merely that it has continued in a well-worn mould which has tended to neglect the more general and objective aspects by concentrating on past origins rather than the existing situation. Within this older framework are to be found certain classic studies of regional settlement geography such as the work by Thorpe (1949) on the green-villages of County Durham and the pioneer surveys by Dickinson (1932, 1934) of the morphology, distribution and functions of market towns in East Anglia. Because each is on a regional basis only and inevitably contains a large element of subjective evaluation, it is not really possible to derive a broad countrywide view from them. Although the consideration of regional differences still involves the process of intelligent assessment, it is both possible and necessary to provide some quantitative estimate of this differentiation before suggesting direct causal variables. The following examination of regional land-use structure in small settlements can contribute part of such a factual base.

HIGHLAND AND LOWLAND ZONE CONTRASTS

Important regional contrasts in the land composition and densities of development in small settlements were first noticed by one of the present authors in his initial work on the subject (Best, 1957 and 1962). At that time, these characteristics could not be explored in depth and, although the differences which appeared to exist between the so-called Highland and Lowland Zones (the north and west as opposed to the south and east of the country) and between different counties were remarked upon, they were not examined to any great extent. Moreover, the nature of the small settlement sample meant that only figures for the total urban area were available, thereby making comparisons between individual urban land uses impossible. A partial breakdown by constituent uses was only available in the very limited additional data for small towns obtained from development plans, but this information referred solely to the four main uses.

These statistical deficiencies, taken together with the fact that the regional theme was only a small part of the research being undertaken, finally resulted in little more than a cursory review being made at that stage. The original findings are still relevant, however, since they provide an indication of the likely trends which might emerge from a more detailed study. Consequently, they are reproduced in Table 17, the data being for the seven counties of the initial sample and also for the special sample from East Sussex.

County	Number of settlements	Mean population size	Mean urban area provision $(ha/10^3p)$
Highland Zone:			
Northumberland	41	920	28·7
Lancashire	36	859	29·0
Monmouthshire	30	2,658	31·3
Devonshire	16	1,867	32·9
Total	123	1,449	30·6
Lowland Zone:			
Lincolnshire (Kesteven)	30	1,130	36·0
Warwickshire	30	973	36·3
Oxfordshire	30	815	39·7
Total	90	973	37·1
Total (all counties)	213	1,348	32·7
East Sussex	39	1,053	53·2

Table 17. Regional variations in the provision of urban land in small settlements, c. 1950

As can be seen from the table, two levels of regional diversifica-
tion were recognised: a primary distinction between the Highland
and Lowland Zones and a contrasting of the data at the county
level. The marked disparity between the Highland and Lowland
Zones of 30·6 ha/1000p and 37·1 ha/1000p, respectively, is
immediately apparent, while, with the counties, there is an
equally clear distinction between the extremes of Northumberland with a relatively low provision (28·7 ha/1000p) and East
Sussex with a very high provision (53·2 ha/1000p). In this latter
case, while there is no reason to doubt the validity of the data, the
the deviation from the norm (c. 32–34 ha/1000p) is so great that
further attention will be given to these figures in the subsequent
discussion. But, for the moment, the most significant point to
note is the divergence between the relatively low land provisions
(i.e. high density) in settlements in the upland north and the high
provisions (i.e. low density) in the lowland south of England,
together with the intermediate provisions in the supposedly
'transitional' counties of Devonshire and Lincolnshire (Kest-
even), for example.

The usual problems encountered when seeking to apply
meaningful regional divisions were augmented in this earlier
investigation by the nature of the settlement distribution which,
in part, resulted from the sampling procedure that had to be
adopted. Even so, it was considered that the two-fold level of
regional treatment described above (i.e. Highland/Lowland
Zones and county divisions) had advantages which merited its
retention in the present study also, albeit with some modifications. The concept of a Highland/Lowland division can be criti-
cised in a number of ways, but only if it is interpreted too rigidly.
As used here with the more recent data for small settlements, it is
merely a device to indicate more clearly the relative contrasts
existing in a particular set of phenomena as they are found in two
broadly distinct environments.

A number of smaller regional groupings of counties has also
been employed, and these divisions were constructed by a largely
subjective process which was based on the distribution of the
sample maps of the Second Land Utilisation Survey (Table 18).

It should be noted that they take no account of the Highland/ Lowland division; and, indeed, two of the groups cross this primary boundary. In this way, it has been possible to gain a good regional spread of land-use data from a variety of areas which reflect the diversity of environments in England and Wales. Some of the groupings in Table 18 contain only small numbers of settlements and should, therefore, be treated with care when statistical comparisons are being made. But examination of these groups suggests no obvious bias in characteristics which might adversely influence any conclusions that may be drawn.

Regional group	Counties	Number of settlements
1. East Kent	Kent	19
2. Hampshire/Isle of Wight	Southampton	13
	Isle of Wight	
3. Oxfordshire/Buckinghamshire	Oxford	27
	Buckingham	
4. East Anglia/Fens	Lincoln (Holland and	37
	Kesteven)	
	Norfolk	
	Suffolk	
5. Staffordshire	Stafford	9
6. South Wales/West Country	Somerset	56
	Gloucester	
	Glamorgan	
	Monmouth	
	Brecon	
	Hereford	
7. North and West Wales	Cardigan	6
	Caernarvon	
8. Lancashire	Lancaster	7
9. Yorkshire	North Riding	75
	West Riding	
	East Riding	
10. North East	Durham	11
	Northumberland	

Table 18. Regional groupings of small settlements

Since the principal object of this chapter is to quantify the regional variations which may exist in small settlement land use, there is clearly a need to discount the influence of other factors which are not strictly relevant in this instance. This particularly applies to the pattern of variation which has been seen to exist with changes in the size of settlements (Chapter 5), a factor that is certainly present at a regional level. As this size variation has been quantified, especially with respect to the provision of urban land, it is possible to allow for this important effect by a consideration of the mean sizes of the regional groupings.

REGIONAL VARIATIONS IN URBAN AREA COMPOSITION

Variations in the composition of the total urban area of small settlements in different parts of England and Wales are far less pronounced than with land provisions, which are dealt with in the next section. The data for the Highland and Lowland Zones and for the regional groups are recorded in Tables 19 and 20. Little variation in the composition of the urban area occurs between the Highland and Lowland Zones as a whole, and the small differences which may be noticed are not significant. Only the proportion under industry would seem to be notably greater in the Lowland Zone.

Zone	Mean popula- tion size	Hous- ing*	In- dustry	Open space	Educa- tion	Four main uses	Residue
				per cent†			
Highland (110)	894	78·9	2·5	11·2	2·5	95·1	4·9
Lowland (150)	920	79·5	4·1	11·6	1·8	97·0	3·0
Overall means (260)	909	79·3	3·6	11·4	2·0	96·3	3·7

* Including commercial land   † Of total urban area

Table 19. The composition of the urban area of small settlements in the Highland and Lowland Zones

At a more detailed level with the regional groups certain features are of interest, although the variation is still small. Some of the below-average figures arise from a higher than average mean size of settlement where the open space element is often larger – as in the north-east. But this explanation is not possible for small settlements in the Hampshire/Isle of Wight and Lancashire groups where, despite a high mean population size, a very large proportion of the urban area (87–90 per cent) is under housing. The data for the other land uses suggest that this situation is

Regional group	Mean population size	Housing*	Industry	Open space	Education	Four main uses	Residue
				per cent†			
North East	1,695	75·5	1·2	17·4	4·2	98·5	1·5
Hants/I.O.W.	1,489	87·2	2·3	6·0	3·2	98·7	1·3
East Kent	1,286	74·5	7·9	12·5	2·4	97·3	2·7
Lancashire	1,268	89·6	3·5	2·8	1·6	97·5	2·5
Oxon./Bucks.	1,189	81·1	3·6	9·8	1·7	96·2	3·8
S. Wales/ West Co.	993	78·7	4·2	11·9	1·5	96·3	3·7
Yorkshire	760	80·3	1·7	9·7	2·0	93·7	6·3
E. Anglia/ Fens	675	73·3	3·8	18·0	1·5	96·6	3·4
N. & W. Wales	361	84·9	–	7·0	5·7	97·6	2·4
Staffordshire	313	79·7	–	14·8	0·5	95·0	5·0
Overall means	909	79·3	3·6	11·4	2·0	96·3	3·7

* Including commercial land   † Of total urban area

Table 20. Regional variations in the composition of urban land in small settlements

probably due to a smaller than average proportion of the urban area being under open space. Conversely, the residential element in the East Anglia/Fens group (73·3 per cent) is certainly smaller than might be expected for settlements of this mean size. In contrast to the Hampshire/Isle of Wight group, this situation is largely because the proportion of open space in these villages is 6·6 per cent higher than the overall mean – a reflection of the straggling nature of many of the settlements in this region which allows a liberal provision of open space between buildings.

Despite such minor variations, the fact remains that there is really little regional difference in the urban area composition of small settlements. The prime function of these settlements, in providing housing rather than other services for the population, is naturally seen throughout the country and, as a result, much regional differentiation in this feature is not to be expected. With individual settlements, of course, variation is fairly common, particularly with large villages and small towns which can sometimes have a sizeable area of industry, open space or land under residual uses. But these special features have a local rather than a strictly regional connotation, even though they may tend to weight the data on urban composition away from the norm. With relatively few exceptions, then, there exists a basic regional uniformity in the proportionate make-up of the urban area in small settlements. It is a circumstance which is not repeated when the provision of land is considered.

REGIONAL VARIATIONS IN URBAN LAND PROVISION

The environmental and cultural factors which may influence the use of land are very evident when differences in the density of urban development are considered. This is especially true of restraints exerted by the natural environment, which even today influence modern building practices and which, in the past, must have been still more stringent in their effects. In particular, the physical controls of slope, relief, climate and hydrology are probably responsible for a considerable part of the significant variations that are seen to exist in land provisions between small settlements in the Highland and Lowland Zones (Table 21). Because of the large size of the two sub-samples used (Highland 110; Lowland 150), and because the mean population sizes of the two groups are so similar, any differences in land provision can be expected to be the result of factors other than that of variation in settlement size. In addition to the environmental constraints, these other factors may well include variations in the economy and function of the settlements concerned, a possibility investigated in the subsequent chapter.

Zone	Mean population size	Housing*	Industry	Open space	Education	Four main uses	Residue	Total urban area
				ha/10³p				
Highland	894	22·7	0·7	3·2	0·7	27·3	1·4	28·7
Lowland	920	30·8	1·6	4·5	0·7	37·6	1·2	38·8
Overall means	909	27·4	1·2	4·0	0·7	33·3	1·3	34·6

* Including commercial land

*Table 21. Variations in the provision of urban land uses in
small settlements in the Highland and Lowland Zones*

Disparities in the density of development are immediately apparent when land used for residential purposes is considered. Provisions in Highland England and Wales are nearly 5 ha/1000p less than the national average (27·4 ha/1000p), while a differential of over 8 ha/1000p exists between figures for the Highland and Lowland Zones themselves. The generally easier and less constraining physical conditions of Lowland England, and especially the greater availability of reasonably extensive tracts of level land for building, may well help to explain the more generous land provision seen there. So, too, may the rather more favourable economic environment and the less dominant legacy of tightly developed nineteenth-century housing. Indeed, the relative disadvantages of the Highland Zone from the economic viewpoint are also suggested by the data for the provision of industrial land (Highland 0·7 ha/1000p; Lowland 1·6 ha/1000p). Much of the urban area recorded as being used for industrial purposes in small settlements is a product of the present century. It is a reflection of a general increase in commercial prosperity eventually

V. Wye, Kent. A sizeable village or small town of about 2,000 people between Ashford and Canterbury. Several buildings near the church date from the 15th century. Considerable expansion since the last war includes a local authority estate in the middle background on the right, and a private development, built since the photograph was taken, on an open field site (middle left).

Aerofilms Ltd.

VI. Burford, Oxford-
shire. A small market
town situated on the
River Windrush. This
view along the main
street illustrates both a
typical Cotswold mar-
ket centre and the
noticeably higher den-
sities than those which
are normally found in
most villages and
hamlets.

Aerofilms Ltd.

reaching rural areas, or else the specific outcome of a policy of industrial decentralisation from larger towns. Both processes have tended to favour Lowland England at the expense of the north and west, and the results are evident from the land provision figures.

As with the housing provision, the regional dissimilarities in the provision of open space in small settlements can again be partially explained by environmental influences. But the low figure for the Highland Zone (3·2 ha/1000p) is also connected with the economic handicaps of the area, the relative lack of prosperity being reflected in poorer facilities in the villages when compared with the Lowland Zone. The distribution of village greens, which can provide an important element in the area of open space in smaller settlements, also helps to explain the divergencies recorded, since the majority of greens are found in the Lowland Zone (Hoskins, 1955; Hoskins and Stamp, 1963). With education, the provision of land in the two zones does not show the discrepancy seen in the case of the other three main uses. The conformity of the figures (0·7 ha/1000p), however, should not be taken completely at face value for it hides differences in physical fabric and social conditions which are very often poorer in upland areas. Furthermore, it will be seen from the detailed regional breakdown that certain irregularities in the provision of educational land are more obvious when analysed at a county level.

Important divergencies in three of the four main uses, therefore, combine to produce overall urban land figures for small settlements which reflect a basic disparity between the Highland and Lowland Zones in England and Wales. Hence, a total urban area provision of 28·7 ha/1000p for the Highland Zone compares with a figure of as much as 38.8 ha/1000p in the Lowland Zone. But within the two zones even greater contrasts exist, and these can be seen quite clearly from the data for the ten regional groups shown in Table 22. In addition, land provision figures for small settlements in East Sussex have been recorded earlier in Table 4.

Unlike the Highland/Lowland divisions, the mean population sizes of these regional groups are, in certain cases, so different

Regional group	Mean population size	Housing*	Industry	Open space	Education	Four main uses	Residue	Total urban area
		ha/10³p						
North East	1,695	14·7	0·2	3·4	0·8	19·1	0·3	19·4
Hants/I.O.W.	1,489	35·5	0·9	2·4	1·3	40·3	0·5	40·8
East Kent	1,286	26·2	2·8	4·4	0·8	34·2	0·9	35·1
Lancashire	1,268	29·1	1·1	0·9	0·5	31·6	0·8	32·4
Oxon./Bucks.	1,189	31·7	1·4	3·8	0·6	37·5	1·5	39·0
S. Wales/West Co.	993	24·4	1·3	3·7	0·5	29·9	1·1	31·1
Yorkshire	760	26·5	0·6	3·2	0·6	30·9	2·1	33·0
E. Anglia/Fens	675	33·8	1·7	8·3	0·7	44·5	1·5	46·0
N. and W. Wales	361	24·4	–	2·0	1·6	28·0	0·7	28·7
Staffordshire	313	34·7	–	6·4	0·3	41·4	2·2	43·6
Overall means	909	27·4	1·2	4·0	0·7	33·3	1·3	34·6

*Including commercial land

Table 22. Regional variations in the provision of urban land uses in small settlements. Data for some groups must be used with caution because of the small size of the sub-samples

from the overall mean that some of the variation in the figures for land provision must be attributed to the size factor examined in the previous chapter. Because the influence of the size factor has been fully analysed, however, it is possible to correct the regional figures to take account of this bias. The calculation of the mathematical functions, and the drawing of the best-fit curves describing the behaviour of certain land provisions over the size range, suggest the land provision figures which might be expected from the regional groupings, bearing in mind the mean population size of each group. When the actual land provisions in the regions differ considerably from the expected figure, as outlined in Fig. 13, then the variations may be ascribed to regional characteristics.

By reference to the size analysis, it is possible to divide the ten regional groups into broad categories depending on whether they show extreme provisions, either high or low, or near-normal provisions. Both the East Anglia/Fens group and the settlements recorded for Hampshire/Isle of Wight, for example, exhibit higher than average provisions for the total urban area (46·0 ha/1000p and 40·8 ha/1000p, respectively), in spite of the fact that the settlements in the latter group have a comparatively high mean population size of nearly 1,500. In the case of this Hampshire/Isle of Wight group, the high total land provision is largely explained by a substantial figure for housing, 35·5 ha/1000p, compared with an estimated mean of about 28 ha/1000p for settlements of this size. There is some evidence to suggest that residential densities in small settlements in southern and south-eastern England are generally of this magnitude, and this figure has strong similarities with the data recorded for East Sussex (Table 4). In contrast, the rather lower residential provision for the East Anglia/Fens group (33·8 ha/1000p) is roughly the average for settlements of about 600–700 people, whereas the provision of open space, 8·3 ha/1000p, is over twice the norm, so again inflating the figure for the total urban area provision. Overall densities of development in eastern England, then, are as open as those recorded for several southern areas, since the straggling nature of many of the villages, particularly in the fenland district, leads to a high provision of open space.

On the other hand, the apparently lower densities of development in southern and eastern England are not confirmed as clearly as might be expected by the small settlements in East Kent, where the land provisions are not very different from the national average. This discrepancy can be partly accounted for by the presence of a component of mining settlements in the sample which tends to lower the provision, particularly with respect to land under housing. The effect will be examined in greater detail in the next chapter. Nevertheless, rural settlement in East Kent probably does not show quite the same general level of low density as recorded for Hampshire, East Sussex and East Anglia, even discounting the influence of extractive industry.

Moving away from southern England towards the north and west, two regional groups, Oxfordshire/Buckinghamshire and Staffordshire, have approximately normal land provisions for their respective mean population sizes. The total urban area provision in the first group is slightly above the expected norm, whereas the residential provision for the Staffordshire group (34·7 ha/1000p) is slightly lower than average. This evidence suggests a general transition in settlement characteristics towards lower land provisions (higher densities) as a progression is made towards the north and west of the country.

In all the remaining regional groups, land provisions are generally lower than might be expected. Although the sub-sample is too small for any differences to be statistically significant, the Lancashire settlements have a remarkably low provision of open space (0·9 ha/1000p), even though the other uses are approximately normal in magnitude. The provision for residential uses in the 75 settlements of the Yorkshire sub-sample is certainly much lower than average – 26·5 ha/1000p for a mean population size of 760 people, when the expected provision should be nearer to 32 ha/1000p. The three other regions which remain all record land provisions well below the average, and it is significant that all three are in upland areas of England or Wales. Although the provision of open space in the South Wales/West Country group is normal, the housing provision (24·4 ha/1000p) is well under the expected mean, while the *relative* residential provision in the western and northern parts of Wales is even lower: statistically it is still 24·4 ha/1000p, but the mean size of settlement is only 361 persons when the expected provision is more of the order of 36 ha/1000p. Finally, the settlements in the north-east of England, in Northumberland and Durham, have residential provisions at a very low level indeed (14·7 ha/1000p). These settlements are generally larger than usual and show a strong urban influence, which, in a number of cases, is related to their function as mining villages. Such factors tend towards a reduction in land provision and lead to the clear regional distinction which is apparent.

When the geographic pattern of small settlements is viewed as a whole, a marked divergence appears to exist in land provisions between the south and east and the north and west of the country, respectively. An intermediate zone occurs in the Midlands. This dichotomy is emphasised by reference to the small settlements of East Sussex where the data, of course, are from a different source. The similarities between East Sussex, on the one hand, and the Hampshire/Isle of Wight and East Anglia/Fens regional groups, on the other, are particularly noticeable, and they indicate that the subjective similarities of village appearance in lowland England have some quantitative basis in fact. It may well be that the small settlements of East Sussex are an extreme form of these conditions which are thought to be fairly general in southern England, with a high residential provision (38·7 ha/1000p) coupled with an open space provision which is twice the national average (7·5 ha/1000p). This results in a total urban provision which is as high as 53·2 ha/1000p.

ANALYSIS OF THE REGRESSION RESIDUALS

The influence of the density-size rule in the present analysis has been minimised by reference to information from the previous chapter. The functions which were obtained in that analysis were those which provided the best explanation for the data, though at a rather low level because of the interference of other factors and, notably, of a regional component which has just been discussed. The effect of the density-size rule has certainly complicated the regional investigation, but it can also be used as a positive aid to further research. This is because it is possible to isolate those settlements which, by the magnitude of their residuals, are less well-explained in terms of the functions resulting from the size analysis. In this way, it can be seen if they show any bias towards other, supposedly causal, influences.

The analysis of the residuals in the regression model providing the highest level of explanation for the size factor shows strong correlation with the regional analysis attempted above. Both positive and negative residuals for all 260 small settlements were listed and these were then related to the standard deviation of the dependent variable – the total urban area provision. In this way, settlements were categorised by whether the residual element varied by an amount which was less than one standard deviation from the best-fit curve, or whether it was 1 to 1·5, 1·5 to 2 or over twice the size of the standard deviation, both positive and negative.

Sixty small settlements recorded residuals in excess of one standard deviation and these are plotted in Fig. 14. A clear pattern of negative residuals in the Highland Zone and of positive residuals in the Lowland Zone is seen. In the former zone, only 7 out of 28 settlements record positive residuals and, of these, 4 are at the lowest level of significance. Conversely, in the Lowland Zone, all but 11 of the 32 settlement residuals are positive, and 9 of these 11 are at the lowest level of variation. Even these exceptions are often explainable. Several such anomalies are found in intermediate regions, such as the West Riding of Yorkshire, Staffordshire and the West Country, which are close to the Highland/Lowland boundary line. Then again, at least one of the settlements in East Kent which shows a negative residual is predominantly a mining settlement.

The concentration of negative residuals in Wales, including six settlements with very high negative values, and also in Northumberland and Durham strongly reinforces the regional data shown in Table 22. There follows an intermediate zone covering the counties of Somerset, Gloucestershire, Staffordshire and the West Riding of Yorkshire where the situation is less clear-cut and where the settlements show transitional elements of both an

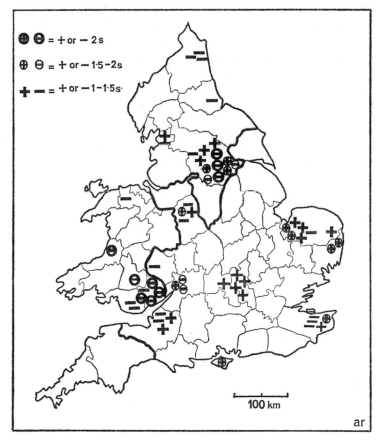

Fig. 14. Regional extremes in small settlement land-use provision: analysis of regression residuals. The Highland/Lowland division is shown by the heavy line

upland and a lowland character. Moving south and east, there are strong nucleations of positive residuals in Oxfordshire, Buckinghamshire, Norfolk and Suffolk where lowland influences are at their strongest.

The analysis of regional variations in the land use of small settlements has certainly augmented both the general picture presented earlier in this study and also the more specific findings of the variation with population size. Naturally, it has been impossible to be precise about the direct causes of the observed regional patterns, but some explanations along the lines of environmental and cultural influences are possible and indeed plausible. Restrictions imposed by relief and slope are especially applicable in Wales and northern England and climatic restraints may be locally important. But, where natural environment influences are not generally admissable as explanations for regional characteristics, reasons can often be suggested in historical and economic terms. The presence of settlements with very definite economic functions, such as mining, was mentioned previously in so far as it helped explain certain regional patterns of land provision. In the next chapter, the importance of the functional role of a settlement in the development of its land-use pattern will be examined further.

7 · Small Settlements and the Local Economy

> 'The nearer we came to Hallifax, we found the houses thicker, and the villages greater in every bottom; and not only so, but the sides of the hills, which were very steep every way, were spread with houses, and that very thick; for the land being divided into small enclosures, that is to say, from two acres to six or seven acres each, seldom more; every three or four pieces of land had a house belonging to it. . . . This division of the land into small pieces, and the scattering of the dwellings, was occasioned by, and done for the convenience of the business which the people were generally employ'd in . . .'
>
> (DEFOE, 1738)

The early growth of the West Riding woollen industry led to radical changes in the settlement pattern of the area as people moved to work in this developing economy. In the passage quoted above, Defoe describes the effects which these movements had upon the landscape; effects which inevitably had an immense influence on the land-use structure of the hamlets and villages surrounding Halifax and the other centres of the new industry. Although these villages had probably existed for nearly a thousand years before Defoe rode through them, the characteristics which he described were largely the product of very recent economic growth. Furthermore, he was describing the landscape in the early 1720s, before the so-called 'Industrial Revolution' can truly be said to have gathered much momentum, and certainly long before the conventional date for the 'take-off' of the British economy, to use Rostow's terminology (W. W. Rostow, 1960), around 1780. By the end of the nineteenth century, after the full effect of Victorian industrial development had been felt, the changing economy had created a completely new landscape in town and village alike throughout many parts of Britain which was as intimately related to the new economic patterns as were the agricultural villages to the old economy of previous centuries.

SETTLEMENT FUNCTION AND HISTORY

Settlements which had grown up to house a population largely dependent on a single source of income had, of course, existed long before the economic diversifications of the last two or three centuries. Sea and river ports and agglomerations of miners' houses were as much a part of Britain as the multitude of agricultural villages and market towns which are traditionally thought of as representing the pre-industrial scene. But the Industrial Revolution crystallised these non-agricultural activities, and the housing of the increased population reflected the new economic and industrial base.

An examination of the relationship existing between the local economy and the land-use pattern of a settlement provides another viewpoint from which small settlement land use can be studied. This will help to complete a picture which has already indicated the regularities which exist with regard to variations in size and in location of settlement. But, as with the regional analysis of the last chapter, there is again a difficulty of quantification which limits the methods of analysis. As will be explained later, statistical indices of economic function are virtually impossible to find even for present day situations, and the problem is made more acute by the need to consider the historical aspects of the local economy as well. Therefore, although surveys of rural industry or rural employment, like that by Robertson (1961), are certainly useful, these studies necessarily deal with modern and sometimes rather ephemeral situations which often do not reflect the economic base that initially gave rise to the land-use complexes under review.

The fact that note must be taken of historical functions presents a further problem: namely, that any such relationship to land use may well have been obscured over the years. For instance, a village originally settled in connection with nearby mining operations, and which a century ago might well have shown the distinctive marks of this influence, could have had the pattern partly obliterated by redevelopment, the growth of additional industrial and service functions, or by the process of suburbanisation and dormitory development in the intervening years. This difficulty, which often leads to the wide variations in land-use conditions found in small settlements, was recognised in the Scott Report (1942). The Committee realised that 'each village had a plan or form related to its function. Since these functions varied widely, since the original siting factor often became unimportant and later additions to an old settlement were consequently governed by other conditions, and since nearly all villages have grown naturally and for the most part slowly, there is today no set pattern to which village plans generally conform – they vary greatly in both shape and size.'

The example of a mining village as a settlement possessing a land-use pattern which is, to a marked extent, functionally orientated makes quite plain the relationship which is being suggested. But, in many cases, this functional orientation is by no means so clear-cut. Starting from rather subjective first principles, it is possible to envisage small settlements as falling into a number of functional types – mining, fishing, agricultural, dormitory, tourist and market settlements, for example. These categories suggest a rather haphazard definition of the concept of 'function' as something reflecting, on the one hand, the original employment structure of the residents (e.g. mining and its associated features) and, on the other, the major 'purpose' of the settlement (e.g. primarily as a residential unit like the dormitory village). Over and above these definitional objections, there will naturally be a difference in the degree to which any particular function influences the land use of the settlement. Whereas the mining influence is invariably strong, for instance, the impact of tourism is usually rather weak.

It should be recognised at this point that the sense in which the term 'function' is now being used is, in many ways, different from that employed by some geographers and economists. Much work, particularly since the Second World War, has been concerned with the interaction of the service functions of a community and the area over which these functions extend their influence. Such work has an important place in regional studies where central place theory and the urban hierarchy are concerned. To take a well-known example, Bracey (1962) has examined the so-called 'functional base' of central villages in Somerset and has recognised three orders of centrality as calculated from the provision of commercial and professional services. Equally, Stafford (1963) has applied a similar mode of analysis to a study of the service functions of 31 small towns in southern Illinois. The links which these studies have with central place theory mean, of necessity, that the service influence of a settlement is considered as paramount; for theorists seek, by examining the service function, to expose a logical rationale for the creation of a pattern of settlements. They are not particularly interested in the specific and often specialised functions of settlements which create 'noise' as far as their theoretical models are concerned and which disturb the regularities that they expose. Yet it is these specific and specialised functions which are primarily of concern here.

In an analysis of this sort, the problems posed by the need for an historical perspective, and the difficulty in obtaining suitably quantified data, invariably lead to a large measure of subjective assessment. A subjective element was particularly present in the original work on the subject (Best, 1957) in as much as the functional type of the settlements in the sample used was decided simply by reference to the professional judgement of the planning officer making the choice of settlements for a particular county. Ten types were detailed: agricultural, industrial, quarrying, transport, dormitory, market, resort, fishing, mining and service. These categories obviously covered a wide range of activities but were not chosen in relation to the historical background or by any quantitative and strictly objective method. This drawback was fully recognised, and, as a result, the analysis of the allotted functional categories was limited simply to a consideration of land provisions in mining and market/dormitory settlements in the two counties of Northumberland and Monmouthshire.

Despite the problems raised by a rather subjective approach, the recognition of mining villages presented few complications, while the dormitory/market classification was justifiably given to somewhat larger settlements where these functions were readily apparent. In the case of the mining settlements in both counties, the mean provision of land for the total urban area was calculated as 15·6 ha/1000p; a very low figure that was related to the extent of tightly developed, company-built housing and the need to cover as little land as possible which might be needed for mining purposes. By way of contrast, the dormitory/market settlements recorded a total provision of 44·9 ha/1000p, nearly three times the mining settlement figure. This largely reflected the relatively recent nature of the dormitory function with the tendency to build at lower densities using a high provision of open space.

Such findings gave firm grounds for thinking that a relationship between settlement function and land-use structure did, in fact, exist. In terms of the present study, however, the subjective classification of settlement functions which was employed was not sufficiently rigorous, and, in consequence, no further analysis of the original sample has been undertaken. As will be seen, however, the analysis of the new data from the Second Land Utilisation Survey has been subject to many of the same problems, and so a somewhat limited approach has inevitably been imposed. There is clearly scope for more detailed research to overcome these difficulties of data insufficiency, perhaps involving case studies of particular settlements.

METHOD OF ANALYSIS

The need to remove as much as possible of the subjective element in the classification of functional types of settlement, and, moreover, the necessity to know the historical background which relates past function to the land patterns which were created at the time, immediately restricts the breadth of the enquiry. Even today it is impossible to quantify satisfactorily the economic functions of a single settlement, despite the seeming superabundance of statistical data, and figures relating to past conditions are almost non-existent. Furthermore, the problem is made no easier by the fact that the Second Land Utilisation Survey maps record only formal land patterns and give little indication of the functional use of land except in very broad terms.

Even if only the present economic structure of settlements is considered, the nature of the data again presents complications. Work at Wye College has investigated the economic structure of certain rural areas in England and Scotland and has attempted to trace the influence of the local employment multiplier in these areas (J. A. Beath, 1968). The data source for this study was the local employment information recorded each year for every employment exchange area and known as Employment Record II (E.R.II). The classification of employment follows the Standard Industrial Classification (1958) in which employees are allocated to one of over 150 industrial groups. In spite of the amount of detail at this scale, however, there is a bar to the further use of these data because the smallest unit for which employment figures are available is the local employment exchange area. If these figures were used in the present study it would be impossible to calculate data for individual small settlements, and settlements which might well be of a very different function would be classified together if they were contained within the same employment exchange area. Still more importantly, since the employment exchange is generally located in a large town or city, the data for any particular E.R.II are strongly biased away from the characteristics of the rural population.

For these reasons, and because present employment statistics often do not provide a good alternative for historical data, it has been impossible to analyse the land-use information as fully as would have been desirable. The primary problem of recognising the major functional characteristics of a particular settlement means that consideration has only been given to cases where there is some degree of certainty, albeit on a somewhat subjective basis. Three important types of evidence have been examined in so far as they can illustrate significant factors influencing the land pattern of small settlements in this country: (a) the presence of manufacturing industry, (b) the special characteristics of mining settlements in particular parts of England and Wales, and (c) a consideration of dormitory influence as being one of the major changes occurring in the present century.

MANUFACTURING INDUSTRY

Of the 260 small settlements in the sample taken from the Second Land Utilisation Survey maps, manufacturing industry was recorded in 57, or just over one-fifth of the total. The more detailed distribution of this manufacturing component is interesting: nearly 30 per cent of all small settlements in the Lowland Zone counties recorded some manufacturing industry, while only 14·5 per cent of the Highland Zone settlements did so. Consequently, it seems that the villages and small towns in the upland and more isolated parts of the country have often been neglected in terms of small-scale industrialisation. Nevertheless, it is evident that, wherever manufacturing industry does occur, there is no significant regional difference in the percentage of the total urban area which it occupies, the proportion averaging about 8 per cent throughout the country. However, this general average naturally hides a wide variation between many individual settlements. There are some with less than 1 per cent of their area under industry, while a few settlements have a very high proportion – like Sandwich, Kent with 31·6 per cent and Wheatacre, Norfolk with 25·8 per cent.

The lowland bias in the distribution of manufacturing industry is matched by a complementary tendency towards a greater amount of industry in the larger small settlements. The mean population size of the industrial sub-sample is 1,852, though perhaps a better measure can be gained from the median size, 1,333. This compares with a median population of 396 for the whole sample of small settlements. It is clear enough, then, that industry favours the larger villages and towns with their more substantial labour supply. With the exception of a few specific industries, notably food manufacturing, flour milling and perhaps the processing of wood and leather, this attraction of manufacturing to the larger small settlements has been predominantly a process of the last hundred years, and particularly a result of decentralisation policies operating since the last war. As a result, the influence of the manufacturing element on the land-use structure of most small settlements has been rather slight, except where the industrial area is extensive enough to influence the total provision of urban land. The small overall effect is seen from the fact that the mean total urban area provision in small settlements containing manufacturing industry is 34·8 ha/1000p, which is very close to the total sample mean of 34·6 ha/1000p. The preponderance of small settlements containing industry within the Lowland Zone, where the total mean urban provision is relatively higher (38·8 ha/1000p), ensures that the influence of the density/size rule on the land provisions is counteracted.

In addition to delimiting the area of land in a particular settlement which is under manufacturing industry, the Second Land Utilisation Survey also records the type of industry. The classification of manufacturing employed follows the form used in the volume of Industrial Tables of the 1951 Census of Population, and the 14 main groupings are detailed in Appendix 2. Of the 57 small settlements in the sample which have industrial land within their urban area, the type of industry is recorded for 53. Of these, 16 have more than one industry located within their boundaries. This latter group invariably comprises the larger small settlements, and the industrial development in them is often the result of planned growth on post-war industrial estates, as, for example, at Thetford in Norfolk. In the majority of cases, however, industry in villages is of one type only and is usually limited to just one establishment.

Appendix 2 also records the occurrences of particular industrial groupings and it is interesting to note the predominance of certain categories of manufacturing in small settlements. The most common grouping is 'engineering, shipbuilding and electrical goods'. Such industries are particularly prevalent in small towns in lowland areas and almost certainly arise from the setting-up of small-scale engineering concerns in rural districts in the post-war period. The next three most frequent groupings are: food, drink and tobacco; manufacture of wood and cork; and treatment of

VII. New Ash Green, Kent. A new village in the North Downs within easy commuting distance of London. An attempt has been made to preserve existing trees wherever possible giving a mature aspect. Nevertheless, the character of development, both in style and space provision, resembles the larger post-war new towns more closely than the typical village of rural England.

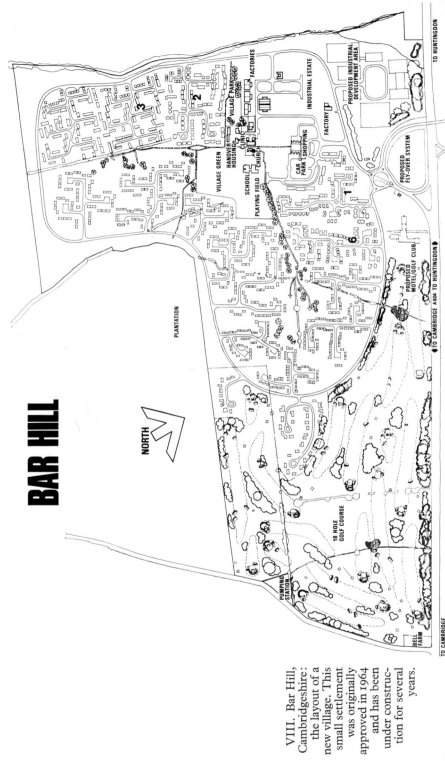

BAR HILL

NORTH

VIII. Bar Hill, Cambridgeshire: the layout of a new village. This small settlement was originally approved in 1964 and has been under construction for several years.

PLANTATION

TO HUNTINGDON

PROPOSED INDUSTRIAL DEVELOPMENT AREA

INDUSTRIAL ESTATE

FACTORIES

FACTORY

PROPOSED FLY-OVER SYSTEM

VILLAGE PARK

HANOVER HOUSING

CLINIC

CHURCH

SCHOOL

VILLAGE GREEN

PLAYING FIELD

CAR PARK SHOPPING

PROPOSED MOTEL/GOLF CLUB

TO CAMBRIDGE A604 TO HUNTINGDON

18 HOLE GOLF COURSE

PUMPING STATION

BELL FARM

TO CAMBRIDGE

non-metalliferous mining products other than coal. All these categories reflect the types of manufacturing which are traditionally associated with industrial development in rural areas. Most of the establishments concerned have their origins in the use of local products and, while the food and wood processing industries may often have lost their original locational advantages, the production of cement, ceramics and other similar goods is still strongly localised with respect to raw material supplies.

COAL MINING

The pit village provides what is probably the clearest example of a functionally orientated small settlement, as well as being an integral part of the rural landscape in certain districts of England and Wales. More than any other form of settlement, it fulfils most emphatically the conditions for functional assessment which were described at the beginning of this chapter. In nearly all cases, the whole urban area was constructed at the same time for a common purpose and frequently by a single organisation – the colliery company. As the firm was concerned solely with the mining of coal, the land-use patterns of mining settlements are seldom complicated by multi-functional origins and developments. As R. T. Jackson has said: 'This singleness of economic purpose led in turn to a distinct form of communal life and to a unique pattern of land use' (in R. P. Beckinsale and J. M. Houston, 1968).

Up to the early nineteenth century, housing for miners in coalfield areas had been largely self-supplied and took the form either of scattered dwellings or else of habitations contained within existing settlements. The development in the last century of company mining brought with it the growth of a capital infrastructure which came to include the provision of housing for the workers if only for the reason that labour had to be attracted to the mines, particularly if these were newly-instituted in areas that were sparsely populated. Especially when new concealed coalfields were opened up, as in Durham in the latter part of the nineteenth century, experienced miners had to be brought to the pit areas and accommodated there. In these circumstances, the provision of housing was an economic necessity for the industrial owners rather than a well-meant demonstration of philanthropy towards the workers.

The first coal-mining villages, built at a time when the mining companies were all-powerful and when the miners had little say in their own living conditions, remain today as the characteristic expression of the nineteenth-century coalfield areas, particularly in the north-east of England. All too often the companies, while providing housing for their employees, stopped short of creating an agreeable environment in which families could live decently. Long, monotonous rows of small terraced houses were plotted out in an unimaginative grid-iron pattern with a minimum provision of urban services, so that, today, these settlements provide a major problem for planners in certain parts of the country (J. R. Atkinson, 1958). The Samuel Commission, reporting in 1925 (Samuel Commission, 1925), gave some idea of the extent of company housing in various parts of Britain in the year of peak coal production, 1913. It was shown that the counties of Northumberland and Durham far exceeded all other areas in the proportion of miner-householders living in houses owned by colliery companies, recording 58·8 per cent and 66·7 per cent, respectively. Even these figures, referring to a total number of about 60,000 houses in the two counties, hide the fact that many villages were entirely constructed by the companies and were therefore completely mono-functional in both their origins and their design (P. H. White, 1951).

A combination of reasons helps to explain the general poverty of conditions in these small settlements. In the first place, despite the early activities of Robert Owen and other philanthropists, the terms 'welfare' and 'economics' were mutually opposed where colliery housing was concerned. Although the provision of housing was necessary to attract labour, the companies provided only the minimum accommodation and facilities, for their main aim was the production of coal and a satisfactory financial return from it – not the provision of housing at good standards or the general encouragement of varied economic growth. Indeed, there was frequently an active discouragement of other commercial expansion within the settlements. In addition, a significant factor contributing to the high housing densities and the generally poor standards of development was the desire of the mining companies to sterilise as little land as possible by urban growth in case future exploitation of the coalfield might be handicapped. Finally, of course, the rows of little terraced houses were often the cheapest form of dwelling to construct and were, therefore, invariably favoured by the companies in the interests of economy.

In the pit villages and small towns of South Wales, two further reasons help to explain the low standards encountered there. The relief of the area, particularly in the rather narrow valleys where many of the miners lived, coupled with the widespread incidence of subsidence and mining damage, meant that building sites were scarce, cramped and often of poor quality. This scarcity led to the activities of housing speculators who were further encouraged by the fact that colliery companies were less active in house construction in South Wales than in some other districts. Indeed, only 12·8 per cent of all miner-householders in South Wales and Monmouthshire lived in colliery-owned houses in 1913.

Although most of the pit villages in the coalfield areas of England and Wales are relict features from the main period of the Industrial Revolution, the latter years of the nineteenth century and the first quarter of the twentieth century saw a further development in this sector. The upsurge of welfare theories and the increased bargaining power of the miners themselves led to the construction of several 'model' colliery settlements which attempted to rectify some of the faults of the earlier versions. Nevertheless, the prime objective of these foundations was still an economic one, as there was a continuing need to attract workers to new pits. But the new settlements went some way towards improving the living conditions of the miners, especially by increasing the allocation of essential services and areas of open space. By and large, the old grid-iron plans were rejected in favour of less stereotyped designs; and the high density terraces, which had been so characteristic of the earlier settlements, were replaced by rather less cramped housing with some provision of garden space.

These changes, many of which were due to the influence of the garden city movement in the early years of the twentieth century, certainly ameliorated conditions in mining settlements, even though the result was sometimes a characterless and uninspired townscape with improvements which were only marginal in their effect.

It is possible to examine in detail the land-use structure of a mining settlement by referring to one of the villages or small towns provided coincidentally by the sample taken from the Second Land Utilisation Survey maps. The place in question is Aylesham in Kent which was constructed entirely as a result of the opening up of the East Kent coalfield after 1913. As the area was completely new to mining operations, skilled labour had to be attracted from other parts of the country. This labour needed to be housed by the colliery companies and, in the event, new villages were constructed to serve all the pits, with the single exception of the Betteshanger mine. In this case, the labour was housed in the newly-constructed Mill Hill estate in Deal. Elvington was built to serve the Tilmanstone pit, while Aylesham was originally conceived as a residential area for two pits, although in fact the second shaft was not sunk and the village became connected solely with the mine at Snowdown.

The influence of the garden city movement is particularly apparent from a study of the plan of Aylesham (Fig. 15), and the specially provided areas of open space and educational land were clearly an attempt to break away from the old patterns. However, many of the space standards associated with this change were in no way commensurate with a radical improvement in living conditions. The arrested development resulting from the failure to open up the second pit meant that the population of Aylesham never reached the projected total of just under 10,000 people, and in 1961 the estimated population was only 4,123. Even with the areas of open space and educational land shown in Fig. 15, the total urban area provision is only 16·7 ha/1000p, while the provision of residential land is 13·3 ha/1000p, or about half the expected norm for a settlement of this size.

There is a total of nine mining villages within the 260 settlements in the Second Land Utilisation Survey sample. Although such a sub-sample is very restricted, it does serve to indicate some of the common characteristics which appear to be associated

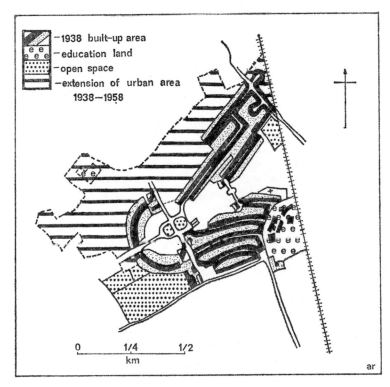

Fig. 15. Aylesham, Kent: the land-use structure of a planned mining village of the twentieth century

with small coal-mining settlements, particularly in respect to relatively high residential densities (Table 23) – which also subsume the commercial provision of land in this instance, it should be remembered. The comparatively tight housing densities are emphasised when the mean residential provision of 14·3 ha/1000p for the sub-sample is contrasted with the average provision of 27·4 ha/1000p for small settlements as a whole. On the other hand, it is interesting to note that the mean residential provision for the small mining settlement is not only rather similar to that of larger towns (small and large town map areas), but is considerably more liberal than the 7·6 ha/1000p found in county boroughs (Table 6), the most populous urban category of all.

Small settlement	County	Population 1961	Residential area*	Residential provision	Total urban area	Total urban area provision
			ha	ha/10³p	ha	ha/10³p
Aylesham	Kent	4,123	54·9	13·3	68·8	16·7
Upton/ N. Elmsall	Yorks (W.R)	5,876	80·1	13·6	111·2	18·9
Askern	Yorks (W.R)	5,701	68·9	12·1	132·8	23·3
Micklefield	Yorks (W.R)	1,844	28·5	15·5	36·4	19·7
Choppington/ Stakeford	Northumberland	8,074	102·4	12·7	124·8	15·5
Pegswood	Northumberland	2,581	34·7	13·4	52·8	20·5
Cambois	Northumberland	2,557	37·0	14·5	48·0	18·8
Netherton	Northumberland	1,394	24·8	17·8	29·0	20·8
Llanelly	Brecon	3,248	74·7	23·0	84·4	26·0
Overall means		3,933	56·2	14·3	76·5	19·5

* Including commercial land

Table 23. The provision of urban land in coal mining settlements of under 10,000 population

Here again, therefore, the operation of the density-size rule becomes very apparent. In small mining villages, the terraced rows of small, tightly-packed houses are often just as characteristic a feature as in the larger mining or industrial towns. But the areal extent of such development is much more confined and is more readily offset or mitigated, in terms of density, by a similarly limited area of housing which may be rather more open in character – whether of older houses on somewhat larger plots or recent estate development at lower densities. The point is made forcibly by comparing the village of Pegswood (Table 23) with

the nearby large settlement of Ashington which had a population
of about 27,000 in 1961. The former settlement has several rows
of old closely-developed terrace housing and a fairly extensive
area of less constricted modern estate housing, giving a composite
residential provision of 13·4 ha/1000p. The latter town, however,
has block upon block of unrelieved by-law terraces in a rigid grid-
iron pattern which give a residential density as tight as 8·6
ha/1000p. There is now some modern estate development on the
fringes of the town, but before this was carried out the urban area
was in a relatively unrelieved nineteenth-century form from the
viewpoint of layout and living space. Moreover, still tighter densities would have been the rule in earlier decades as the population
of the town has been declining.

This comparison of space standards, however, should not be
seen as implying that the living conditions found in small
mining settlements are reasonably adequate. On the contrary, of
the nine settlements in the sub-sample, all but two have more
than 5 per cent of their population living at densities greater than
1½ persons/room. In fact, in five cases, the proportion is 10 per
cent or more, with Pegswood and Netherton in Northumberland
recording the very high figures of 21·3 per cent and 14·3 per cent,
respectively. These proportions are to be compared with a mean
figure of only 2·3 per cent for Rural Districts of England and
Wales in 1961. Clearly, the extremes in living space standards
can be found within the small settlement category alone.

DORMITORY GROWTH

If the land-use pattern of many small mining settlements has
largely been the result of major constructional development over
a very limited period of time, most other small settlements have
tended to grow in a far more piecemeal fashion as a result of a
multitude of individual decisions lacking the rigid control of a
single authority. In recent years, the increasing separation of
workplace from residence has become a notable social pheno-
menon, and this trend has been paralleled by a growth and spread

of dormitory functions in many small settlements located within comparatively easy commuting distance of cities and large towns (J. Whitehand, 1967). Essentially, this particular type of development has also been piecemeal in character, though now carried out within the limitations imposed by post-war planning legislation.

Just as the urban and industrial development of the nineteenth century was focussed on the coalfields and was, in part, responsible for the creation of the mining settlements already described, so in the present century it is possible to consider the growth of dormitory settlements as a major characteristic of the process of modern urbanisation (F. I. Masser and D. C. Stroud, 1965). As Chisholm (1958) has pointed out, most villages within the radius of several miles from a prosperous town have gained in population from an influx of people who commute daily to their workplaces in the town and return home again at night. In itself, this process is a reflection of a rising level of affluence coupled with greatly improved transport facilities which make these daily movements technically possible. But, increasingly, the economic and technological reasons behind dormitory development are being replaced by social motivations which ascribe a certain quality to country living and so encourage residential location in country areas.

The origins of dormitory growth are now at least a century or more old. The great increase in personal mobility brought about by the development of railways, especially after 1870, was particularly notable in the London area. Here, the location of new stations on the network of lines radiating from the metropolis had a strong influence on the pattern of suburban dormitory expansion. After the First World War, the improvement of the motor vehicle further increased the ease with which people could travel between home and a distant workplace, and, at least as far as the London area was concerned, the same period also saw the electrification of many of the rail links with the capital and the extension of the zone within which commuting was thereby made feasible. This trend has continued unabated since 1945, particularly with the rise in car ownership which has increased threefold since the pre-war period (C. Buchanan, 1962). Naturally, this process now involves all major urban areas and not just the metropolis itself.

Commuting and the associated increase in dormitory develop-ment are now characteristic of a broad social spectrum, but the first developments in the late nineteenth and early twentieth centuries were generally the preserve of the higher income groups alone. Therefore, the movements at this time towards residential areas well away from London were dominated by the well-to-do who sought to escape from urban congestion by living in the country. There was also a strong economic motive involved, as well as social considerations, since there was every incentive to invest in property at that time. An interesting illustration of this tendency is seen in Galsworthy's novel, *The Man of Property* (1906), where he recounts the decision of Soames Forsyte to invest some of his capital in a house at Robin Hill: 'The times were good for building, money had not been so dear for years . . . Within twelve miles of Hyde Park Corner, the value of the land certain to go up, would always fetch more than he gave for it; so that a house, if built in really good style, was a first-class invest-ment'.

As such housing was associated with a wealthy class and was built as much as an investment as a domicile, it is not surprising that early dormitory expansion was frequently characterised by an extensive use of land. Houses tended to be large, with gardens often half a hectare or more in extent, so that residential densities were sometimes very low in many villages around London. By comparison, later dormitory development, particularly after the First World War, was generally on a more intensive scale as it was built to meet a demand from a less wealthy but far more numer-ous public whose main concern was to gain a home rather than a good investment. But, if land provisions at this time were less generous than in certain earlier suburban situations, they were still much more liberal than in most inner residential districts of existing towns. In consequence, the actual area over which subur-ban growth now occurred was proportionately far greater than with most previous urban expansion. This outward surge was made possible by increased personal mobility and affluence, which were complemented by the availability of cheap land for building resulting from the depressed state of agriculture and the virtual absence of planning controls. Even with the institution of such controls after the Second World War, the expansion of many dormitory villages continued, for legislation has generally aimed at influencing the form and layout of development rather than simply restricting its total extent.

The difficulties associated with the recognition of the functional character of small settlements, which were mentioned earlier, become even more complex when the influence of dormitory growth on land-use structure and provision is considered. In the first place, such growth is often incorporated in, or appended to, an existing settlement of some antiquity, so that the effect is partly submerged in any consideration of total land provisions. Yet, even when dormitory development appears to have been responsible for almost the whole area of a small settlement, it is normally not easy to recognise such a function by purely objective evaluations because of the lack of detailed statistics for journeys to work in small towns and villages. In contrast to small mining settlements, therefore, it has been impossible to draw a proper sub-sample of dormitory settlements.

In spite of this handicap, however, some generalised conclusions about the land-use structure of dormitory settlements can be made by recourse to less rigorous and more qualitative assessments. It is highly likely, for instance, that many of the small settlements in East Sussex, and particularly those in the north of the county, show characteristics which are due to dormitory growth. Invariably, a relatively open density seems to be one such feature. But fortunately in East Sussex, it is also helpful to find that the county planning authority has collected information on the proportion of the resident population finding employment outside certain settlements, thereby giving some quantitative indication of dormitory function. Six such dormitory settlements and their total urban area provisions are recorded in Table 24. Of these, the settlement of Willingdon (population 2,629), for example, had over 77 per cent of its employed population working outside its confines at the time of survey. It recorded a total land provision of 43·1 ha/1000p which is well in excess of the provision normally associated with a place of this population size. Indeed, a total urban land allocation of over 20 per cent more than the mean figure to be expected under the density-size rule seems to be a feature of most small dormitory settlements.

Small settlement	Population	Total urban area	Employed population working elsewhere*
		ha/10³p	per cent
Hassocks	3,203	37·1	71
Willingdon	2,629	43·1	77
Ringmer	1,476	42·9	49
Westfield	690	47·0	67
Amberstone	165	38·0	84
Shovers Green	27	141·5	78

* Outside the stated settlement

Table 24. The provision of urban land in certain dormitory settlements of under 10,000 population in East Sussex in about 1954

In the absence of adequate basic data for small dormitory settlements as a group, it may be instructive to examine the development of a single example which appears to reflect some of the features of dormitory growth already remarked upon. J. T. Coppock (in J. T. Coppock and H. Prince, 1964) has studied in some detail the development of Radlett in Hertfordshire from the early 1890s. With the coming of the railway in 1868, the hamlet expanded away from its old centre and developed afresh near the new railway station. Although growth was only moderate up to the outbreak of the First World War, it was nevertheless significant that there were distinct differences in land use and residential development which were correlated with the social structure of the expanding settlement. By 1914, a third of the houses in Radlett had been built for well-to-do commuters to London who had moved out of the city both to gain a country home and to invest in property. These houses were detached and spacious and were generally situated in a large garden of about a tenth of a hectare. Consequently, the residential provision for these parts of the village was around 30 ha/1000p (10 houses per ha). This was a very liberal allocation and was in distinct contrast to the areas of terraced houses and cottages, which had been built to serve the population working locally, and which were developed at residential densities of only about 6 ha/1000p (50 houses per ha).

The major period in the expansion of Radlett was between the wars when the commuting element increased enormously and two-thirds of all the dwellings erected were detached houses bought by owner-occupiers. But only one-third of these detached houses were large residences, built at a provision of about 30 ha/1000p as in the pre-1914 period. At the same time, another social change was seen in the construction of 78 semi-detached and terraced houses by Watford Rural District Council for tenant occupation. The availability of land for building and the general absence of planning controls in the 1930s was exemplified by the plans to develop the Newberries estate. This was to be a type of 'garden village' which would be attractive to middle income commuters. The plans envisaged a residential density of about 20 ha/1000p (15 houses per ha) – still a very liberal provision and indicative of the spacious standards of much suburban growth at that time (Best, 1965 and 1968). However, little house-building had actually taken place here before war broke out. When development eventually proceeded again after the Second World War, the influence of the new planning regulations, and particularly of green belt legislation, was seen by the fact that the residential provisions were substantially reduced to 12 ha/1000p (25 houses per ha). This trend towards higher densities has continued to the present time, particularly as there has been an increase in the amount of building by the local authority at somewhat restricted space standards.

Radlett, now with over 8,000 inhabitants, tends to characterise the changing effect of commuter influence over the last century. It shows the early stimulus provided by the new railway and the influx of wealthy house-owners eager for a country home. There was then a shift in social emphasis as dormitory living became the province of the middle classes and the general concern for community welfare caused the construction of council estates in the expanding villages. More specifically, Radlett reflects in its varying residential space standards many of the changes which have been characteristic of much of English suburbia over the last century: the liberal land provisions associated with the housing of wealthy businessmen commuting in the 1890s, the relatively expansive use of land for housing related to the *laissez-faire* attitudes of the 1930s, and the more controlled and less sprawling nature of dormitory development since 1945.

8 · Decline and Revitalisation

For a thousand years English rural life has been a closed system – a stable amalgam of family ties and social patronage, of grass root economics and strictly limited geographical mobility. But within the last half century there has been a swift and fundamental change, and the system is now no longer closed. This radical alteration has influenced the whole English countryside and particularly the villages and market towns which are, in many ways, the most tangible expressions of the old order. The disintegration or undermining of both the old social structure and the long-established local economy, frequently based on agriculture, have pulled in two directions: rural settlements have often declined in socio-economic standing compared with cities and towns but, more recently, they have increasingly become an adjunct of growing importance to larger urban areas because of their newly-developed dormitory functions. Either way, there has been a replacement of patterns and traditions which have lasted hundreds of years by a new set of circumstances. As Sharp (1946) has commented: 'The decline of the village tradition has been clearly reflected in the change in the physical character of many of the older villages and in the form and character of the additions which have been made to them.'

CHANGES IN ECONOMIC AND SOCIAL STRUCTURE

Until about the beginning of the last century, the conditions which Sharp has typified as the 'village tradition' presented a stable and secure aspect which seemed as immutable as the existence of the land itself. Yet already the forces which have collectively undermined the basis of this system were in existence. The influence of the new economic pressures of the Industrial Revolution were seen in the previous chapter to have had a specific effect on land-use structure in individual settlements; but, in addition, they had a general and far-reaching impact which eventually destroyed the old regime in its entirety. This process has perhaps been most evident with rural depopulation and the general movement of many of the agricultural population to the manufacturing industry of the towns, especially during the latter part of the nineteenth century (J. Saville, 1957). Particularly since the Second World War, however, this depopulation process has been reversed in many areas and, rather than losing people, many villages and small towns have in fact increased in size with the influx of an adventitious population. Indeed, since 1951 the population of Rural Districts in England and Wales has grown by well over 1·5 million persons (Ministry of Housing and Local Government, 1967). But this changeabout should not be exaggerated in its extent, for in many districts, and particularly in upland and remote regions, the progress of depopulation has been continuous and unrelieved.

Moreover, one significant element often associated with the depopulation process remains, even in areas near to the conurbations where villages may now be gaining in overall population. This factor is the decline in the importance of agriculture as an employer of the rural labour force. In 1851, 1·48 million people were employed in agriculture in England and Wales. By 1945, the continuation of depopulation, mechanisation and rising labour productivity had resulted in a decline in the regular farm labour force to 616,000, while by 1966 the figure had dropped to only 295,000 (Ministry of Agriculture, Fisheries and Food, 1968). Therefore, a two-sided picture of the demographic structure of rural England and Wales emerges, with some areas showing a persistent loss of population while others are gaining from a twentieth-century inflow of people. In many parts of the country, and especially in lowland England, these patterns of decline and growth are often closely mixed together, and such a situation has been examined by Valerie Jackson (1968) in her study of the population structure of the North Cotswold Rural District in Gloucestershire.

Such basic changes in rural population and the rural labour force have been paralleled by related alterations in the economic structure of rural areas. In many cases, these are a direct result of radical improvements in transport and mobility, particularly since the coming of the railways and, more recently, of the motor car. The self-contained nature of villages and hamlets in the past arose largely because the majority of inhabitants could obtain nearly all their essential requirements within the settlement, while extra needs and additional luxuries could be satisfied by an occasional visit to the nearby market town or by using the local carrier who provided an important service link between village and town. Until the arrival of modern travel facilities, most country people had either to walk or, if they were fortunate, to use horse transport to get about – methods which had been in existence since the foundation of the villages themselves. Consequently, it is not unexpected to find that the rural settlement pattern in this country grew up as a direct response to this limited mobility of the country population in past centuries.

In many lowland areas of England, market towns developed at about 10 to 13 km apart, which meant that, at the most, the inhabitants from an intervening village would not have to travel above 13 km per day on the journey to and from market. This pattern is particularly clear in East Anglia which, as a populous and prosperous agricultural region with few physical handicaps to the growth of settlements, produced a network of market centres to serve the local economy. The decrease in the widespread marketing function of towns and villages in this area from the sixteenth century to the present time has been admirably illustrated by R. E. Dickinson (1932) in his classic study of the smaller urban settlements of East Anglia. He attributes much of the decline in market towns which occurred before the coming of the railways to the improvement in road transport, especially after about 1780, and to the gradual disappearance of the local woollen industry. In addition, several districts, notably Breckland and the Suffolk coastline, were economically backward and, as such, were incapable of maintaining a full complement of urban services and functions. The advent of rail transport further accelerated the process of rationalisation and so removed the *raison d'être* for many of the small towns of the region.

The final breakdown in the traditional local economy has occurred in the present century and has again been associated with increased personal mobility and improvements in transportation. But, while the functions of many small settlements have declined over the last three or four hundred years, the settlements themselves are still in existence. From the economic and social viewpoint, the role of these places has changed, but in the physical sense they remain as relict features of previous economies.

This anomalous situation is one of the key problems in an understanding of the English countryside now and in the future. The extent of this discrepancy between past purpose and present function has been estimated roughly by G. P. Wibberley (1965) and his opinion is worth recording: 'If the modest assumption is made that the average radius served effectively by a market town under present day conditions is only double what it was in the days of horse transport, this means that approximately 75 per cent of existing country towns are no longer necessary for their original purpose. The remaining 25 per cent should be sufficient to satisfy the functions of a market town in the twentieth century serving a modern and highly mobile agricultural industry.' In terms of the market town as an agricultural service centre, there is little doubt that such an assessment is true enough. Indeed, it is not unreasonable to suggest that the figure of 25 per cent which has been quoted would be even smaller if it were not for the fact that many agricultural services still remain on a relatively local basis. This is particularly true of such activities as the retailing of agricultural machinery and the trade in cereals; the one is very much a descendant of the old blacksmith's trade while the other is still orientated towards the local corn merchant, even though he may now be part of a national combine.

The suggestion that the settlement pattern of England and Wales is outdated, and is no longer operating under its original conditions, sometimes stimulates a strong reaction from those concerned with the preservation of English rural life. Yet a largely emotional response such as this often completely misses the point at issue; namely, that the old settlement functions have been changing and are being replaced by new functions which are not too easily recognisable at first. But this different economic footing, coupled with the relative permanence of urban land, can result in the continued existence of market towns and villages which would otherwise decline and decay. It is interesting to observe that the supposed defence of the English country town or village, when vigorously expressed in print, does not usually come from the type of person who has lived in these places for centuries. Rather it comes from the new, twentieth-century types of resident. Their attitudes are symptomatic of a general reversal of opinion about life in the countryside, for, whereas the town dweller once regarded the country as bereft of civilisation and culture and the home of 'rude mechanicals', he now views it more as a desirable retreat from urban stresses and a place to which he can escape in his retirement, if not before.

Shifts in the economic structure of rural areas, and the alterations in viewpoint just referred to, have together brought about a further change in the social structure of small settlements. The concern of the townsman for the fate of the villages and small towns is not simply an impersonal and altruistic interest in rural problems by themselves, but rather a well-founded desire to see his own ideal environment remain in its original form. No longer is the population of the village composed solely of agricultural labourers, farmers, a few shopkeepers and a mixed group of gentry and aristocracy, as portrayed by Flora Thompson (1945) in *Lark Rise to Candleford*. All these groups are now in a minority, and their place has been taken by workers from nearby towns and, more recently, by commuters to the city.

R. E. Pahl (1966) has studied this change, and it is relevant to record his findings. He recognises, in a hypothetical village in the south-east of England, eight main social groups:

1. Large property owners – a relic of former times and not numerically important.
2. Salaried immigrants with some capital.
3. 'Spiralists' – defined as employees of large-scale organisations who live in the village and commute daily to town.
4. Those with limited income and little capital.
5. The retired.
6. Council house tenants.
7. Tied cottagers and other tenants.
8. Local tradesmen and owners of small businesses.

Of these groups, only the first and the last two are remnants of the old social order, and none is particularly significant in absolute numerical terms. More specifically, Pahl (1964a and 1965b) has studied the new social structure of certain settlements in Hertfordshire as it has been influenced by the metropolis, and he has particularly traced the effect of the influx of commuters on village life.

Although the changed social structure of villages and small towns in this country is not of direct concern to this study, it is important indirectly for the future of land use in small settlements. As we have seen, in terms of land-use planning there has been a tendency to neglect rural areas and to concentrate attention on the towns. But this emphasis is now beginning to shift. Small settlements in many areas are no longer the backward retreats of an otherwise advanced nation; rather they are increasingly becoming an essential part of urban life and society and must be considered in this way. Ideas which are rooted in outdated concepts of the nature of the rural community have little part to play in such a new assessment. G. P. Wibberley (1960) has summed up this social change in the following way: 'In the middle of this twentieth century we are uncertain as to what is really meant by the term 'rural community' and whether there are now any significant differences between rural and urban people in the life they live, in their hopes and aspirations and in their attitudes and mores.'

Both this uncertainty and the previously mentioned need for a positive approach to the future of rural settlement are due, in part, to developments since 1945. Therefore, before some tentative suggestions for rural planning in this context are discussed, it will be necessary to review certain of the changes which have occurred in the post-war period.

SOME POST-WAR TRENDS

Wars are traditionally regarded as times of social ferment and as opportunities for ideological catharsis. Consequently, it is not to be wondered at that, following both world wars in the present century, there have been strong movements demanding improvements in the general environment of the population. The First World War brought forth the call of 'homes fit for heroes' while the Second World War provided the real starting point for the present general concern with land-use planning. English rural settlement has been no exception to this pattern. Perhaps the threat of invasion and deprivation forced an awareness of the countryside which, in one respect, degenerated into an unproductive romanticism and, on the other, provided a footing for definite proposals regarding rural land use.

A mixture of both these approaches can be seen in the Scott Report (1942), where changing rural conditions and viewpoints were first given official recognition. The underlying attitudes of the members of the Committee were examined in Chapter 1, and, even if their premises may now be considered mistaken in certain respects, their concern was laudable in its intent and perhaps symptomatic of a changed outlook. In the following year, for example, a conference was held jointly by the Town and Country Planning Association and representatives of local authorities to consider the future of the English country town (S. Baron, 1943). The recommendations were characteristic of the climate of opinion at that time. The need to protect the rural heritage was stressed, while suggestions were made for industrial and population development in certain small towns – recommendations which strongly reflected the attitudes of the Scott Report and also the ideas put forward by the Barlow Report in 1940. These concepts were later incorporated in legislation as part of the New Towns Act of 1946 and the Town Development Act of 1952 and were an integral part of the mechanism by which green belt policy was intended to work.

The whole body of planning infrastructure which has grown up since 1945 has provided one of the major influences on post-war change in rural areas in as far as it has given a legal sanction for such processes as industrial decentralisation, dormitory growth and overspill. Yet much of the legislation since 1945 until the present time has been based on attitudes which began to mature in the 1940s. As far as rural areas were concerned, these attitudes rested on two main articles of faith: one was a desire to revitalise the countryside by encouraging controlled settlement growth and industrial expansion, and the other was to demarcate once and for all those areas which were regarded as 'country' from those considered as 'town'. Both ideals followed naturally from conditions in the 1930s. A depressed agriculture had then encouraged the hope of a more prosperous countryside in the future, while the stressing of the urban/rural dichotomy was a natural reaction against the ribbon development and the suburban sprawl of the inter-war period.

The ideal of a clear urban/rural distinction was, in point of fact, formalised in the Green Belt Act of 1938. The concept was strengthened by the Greater London Plan (1944), which attempted to limit the growth of the metropolis, and was further enshrined in the principles of the New Towns Act of 1946. With small settlements, there has been a policy of strict control of development, infilling and accretion which has been administered by local planning authorities under the provisions of the 1947 Town and Country Planning Act.

The process of rural revitalisation has been centred mainly on the small market town (see, for example, K. S. Woods, 1968). In many cases, these country towns received a wartime employment boost from an enforced industrial decentralisation policy. This trend was to some extent continued after the war, and was positively aided by the Town Development Act of 1952, under which specific agreements were encouraged between large urban centres and small towns for the export of population and industry to offset some of the problems of congestion. By and large, however, the Act dealt with settlements in excess of 10,000 people (D. I. Scargill in Beckinsale and Houston, 1968), although some small settlements did in fact receive overspill population. Thetford in Norfolk was such a settlement where, in 1954, a proposal was made to accept 10,000 people from London, but this arrangement was later modified to deal with only 5,000 people. Families, mainly from the Bethnal Green area, began to arrive after 1959. A trading estate was built to provide employment for the increased numbers and, by 1961, twenty-two firms were in operation, generally employing between ten and twenty workers each.

As well as specific industrial developments on newly-established estates in expanded towns, there has also been a general increase in rural employment since 1945. A study conducted by the Agricultural Economics Research Institute at Oxford, for example, calculated a total employment gain in rural areas of 19 per cent in the period 1953–58 (G. H. Peters, 1962). The labour force involved in such job-expansions has been obtained invariably from the immediate locality and is often housed on new estates and council housing developments which have grown up since the war. Small-scale population growth on such estates has been characteristic of many rural settlements and presents a striking change from the general trend of rural decline seen in so many areas during the 1930s. C. S. Orwin (1945) examined a part of north Oxfordshire in which all the villages had shown a decline of population in the period 1881 to 1931. When the same nineteen villages were resurveyed in the 1960s (M. Robinson, 1963) the trend had been reversed, especially in the larger villages, even though the decline in agricultural employment had continued unchecked.

The population growth of villages in areas such as the north Cotswolds cannot be explained simply as the dormitory expansion of small settlements around London. Nevertheless, a dormitory element certainly exists, and labour moves daily from the villages of north Oxfordshire to work in the offices and factories of

Birmingham, Banbury and Oxford as well as in the departments and colleges of the university. Such previously remote areas are particularly subject to altered social patterns which have given them a new and different lease of life. For one thing, the trend towards increased amounts of leisure, allied with growing affluence, has stimulated an important demand for week-end cottages and second homes in general. In many respects, it would seem that this country is following the trend seen especially in Scandinavia where rural areas are benefiting to some extent from an influx of population which is truly adventitious. On the other hand, these people are, in a sense, only temporary residents.

THE IMPACT OF PLANNING

Population growth and industrialisation, overspill and planning have all radically changed the character of many small settlements in the last quarter of a century. But while the population expansion in rural districts of over two million persons can be used as a partial indicator of change, the related alterations in land use have been as much in quality as in quantity. Qualitative change in the human environment is very difficult to measure, and it is reasonable to contend that there are no absolute standards by which such trends may usually be judged. Nevertheless, much of the post-war development in small settlements has, by any standards, been ill-designed and out of character and has been subjected to considerable and justifiable censure.

The implementation of post-war planning policy, as far as many villages and small towns are concerned, has generally been either by a process of 'judicious infilling' of the existing village plan or else by a modest expansion, involving the construction of small 'estates' of council housing or, more recently, of privately-built homes. Both methods are capable of gross misuse and can result in what Lionel Brett has called 'village idiocy'. In another context he has examined in detail this tendency towards qualitative degeneration by the use of specific examples. In his book *Landscape in Distress*, Brett (1965) reviews post-war development and planning in southern Oxfordshire and traces the effects of expansion and overspill in both a village, Chalgrove, and a small town, Thame. Of the former settlement, he says: 'In all forms of development, the first act has been to tear down all rural back-cloth, willow trees, hedges, bulldozing banks formed by the old lanes, turning ditches into piped culverts, laying down of kerbs and tarmacadam footpaths. . . . In all the new development and proposals, the layout has been a standard plot layout, sub-dividing the land around hammer-head culs-de-sac, or loop roads. . . . Not only the wrong thing in the wrong place, but the wrong thing anywhere.' All too often, it would seem, rural planners have succeeded in providing better living standards, which are a credit to post-war social welfare policies, but un-fortunately they have done this at the expense of 'the wrong thing in the wrong place'.

The absence of detailed time-series information about urban land use in small settlements has meant that any quantitative estimate of post-war change is almost as difficult to make as a qualitative assessment. Theoretically, the 1947 Town and Coun-try Planning Act made provision for the quinquennial review of development plan town maps, including those of under 10,000 population. If local planning authorities had been able to keep strictly to this timetable, there might by now have been at least some statistical information on small towns which would have allowed a proper, if limited, time-series analysis. But, for very good reasons, planning authorities have often been rather tardy in reviewing their plans, especially for small town map areas. As a result, land-use information in this respect is very incom-plete and analysis can only be on a restricted basis.

Nevertheless, a study of the existing material was carried out by M. W. Bruce (1967) at Wye College and his findings are very relevant to this study as they provide the only quantitative data presently available. He analysed development plans and reviews submitted to the Ministry of Housing and Local Government which referred to the period from about 1950 to 1960. An attempt was made to assess the change in urban land use in several settlement categories in England and Wales between these years;

but, because of the low priority given to rural settlement, this particular sector was the most difficult to investigate. Some figures were of use, however, though in total they only represented nine small town map areas which recorded the land-use changes occurring over the required period. Not only was this sample far too small to admit of any statistical accuracy, but it also referred to settlements which, by the very fact of their choice as town map areas, had certain special characteristics. The mean population size, for instance, was nearly 6,000 persons. Yet, in the absence of any other information, these data should at least be recorded.

Within the period under review, the mean increase in the total urban area of the settlements concerned was of the order of 23 per cent, or in absolute terms, 52 ha. Although the sample is clearly irrelevant for representing changes in villages and hamlets, it is not unreasonable to suppose that an increase of this magnitude is indicative of the changes in quite a few small towns, particularly in lowland England. With regard to densities of development, a trend can be observed towards a more liberal provision of land for all uses. Of a total mean increase in the provision of urban land from 32·3 ha/1000p to 37·6 ha/1000p, over half (2·9 ha/1000p) represented a growth in the residential provision and about one quarter (1·3 ha/1000p) in the residual provision. From this evidence, it is clear that fairly recent extensions in the area of small towns, and particularly of their residential land, have been at relatively lower densities than those associated with the existing urban area.

These conclusions about small town map areas, however, are not generally applicable to the majority of small settlements. Undoubtedly, many villages have seen little or no growth since the war, let alone an increase of nearly one quarter of their total area. For alterations in land provisions, too, these development plan data are largely inappropriate. As building in many villages has not involved extensions to the boundary of the settlement, but has more often been concerned with a rather limited infilling of gaps within the urban area, provisions of residential land have probably decreased in many cases. Even when new rural estates have actually been built in villages, the same trend probably applies since existing densities in villages are considerably lower than those in small towns (see Chapter 5) and the new development, therefore, may well be at comparatively higher densities.

Although comprehensive legislation has been enacted several times since 1947, the Town and Country Planning Act of that year provided the basis for rural settlement planning as it now exists. It called for the appraisal of existing conditions and proposals for future policy to be set out in a development plan at the county level, supplemented by town maps produced in greater detail for individual settlements of importance from the planning point of view. As already seen, some settlements of under 10,000 population have had a town map prepared for them, but the vast majority have not been treated in this way. The latter have often been situated in so-called 'white' areas, where little change in land use is expected, and away from the towns and cities which are of prime concern to the local planning authority. But sometimes such small settlements are found within an official or unofficial green belt surrounding a much larger urban settlement and so receive rather more attention from the planners. Even then, however, the planning of a village or small town is usually considered only in relation to the nearby and dominant urban centre and not on its own merits.

By and large, villages located within 'white' areas have only been planned to the extent that individual building developments may have been controlled. Little thought has been given to their overall plan or to their regional role. For villages in green belt areas, however, the Ministry of Housing and Local Government (now Department of the Environment) directed local authorities to select certain settlements for special surveys and the production of village maps at the $2\frac{1}{2}$-inch scale, but only if substantial development was expected to take place within the settlements concerned (Mandelker, 1962). In all other cases, green belt villages have generally been treated as if they were in the 'white' areas, where a policy of development restriction and control has been followed rather than one of positive planning. For the most part, therefore, decisions regarding small settlements have been made on an individual, *ad hoc* basis: a private applicant wishing to build in a village has had his application considered by the local planning authority without any regard for an overall village policy since no such policy normally existed. Even if the authority has had some guidelines for development, these were probably based only on the county development plan outline referring to its rural areas which has almost invariably been of a rather general, non-specific character and capable of several interpretations. The basic fact remains that the planning procedure evolved since 1947 has been strongly orientated towards dealing with the problems of larger settlements with the result that country areas have either suffered by relative neglect or else have been subject to a policy formulated for different circumstances.

This deficiency in land-use planning in this country has been recognised by several planning authorities, and a few attempts have been made to develop a better rural planning policy at the local level (A. Thorburn, 1971). In most instances, such a policy is integrated with the development plan, and the fairly recent reviews of these plans in certain counties show a greater awareness and more detailed treatment of the problems of country-side planning than did the first submissions in the early 1950s. For example, the first development plan for Cambridgeshire in 1952 put forward a general policy for the development of rural settlement which suggested that a ring of villages around Cambridge should be expanded to deal with an additional population of 7,500, while certain villages at greater distances from the city were singled out as growth points for the future (Anon., 1966). When the plan was reviewed subsequently, this policy was expanded to include more detailed investigations of the rural settlements themselves, and so-called 'policy plans' were produced for 120 villages in the county.

Probably one of the most thorough-going policies of this kind is the strategy implemented by the county planning department of East Sussex, which has tried to go further than the simple construction of a planning policy for a limited number of its rural settlements. Within the county, all small settlements have been surveyed and classified according to the planning procedures considered to be most suitable for the settlement, and a conscious attempt has been made to integrate areas of new development into the existing rural environment (L. S. Jay, K. D. Fines and J. Furmidge, 1965). Moreover, the East Sussex authority includes within its planning procedures a complete survey of the rural social structure of the county as an aid to decision-making, and this pattern has been followed in other counties such as Kent and Hampshire (see, for example, Hampshire County Council, 1966).

The fact that several planning authorities stand out as having made a conscious effort to formulate policies to suit their rural areas shows that the approach to the post-war planning of small settlements has not been entirely negative. Where more positive attitudes exist they have, in the main, reflected one of two approaches. Most commonly, a programme of selective expansion of certain settlements has been planned with the intention that these settlements should become rural growth points. Other villages and small towns have been scheduled for limited growth, while the remainder are theoretically not to be allowed to grow at all. Less frequently, a second and more ambitious policy has been considered. This is the construction of completely new villages to house an expanding rural population without having the problem of integrating the new areas of housing development into the existing village matrix, as with normal proposals for expansion. Whether either policy provides a really satisfactory solution to village planning problems is debatable. But what is certain is that both policies are being implemented and are, therefore, of concern here to the extent that they are influencing the structure of land use within small settlements.

SELECTIVE EXPANSION AND DECLINE

Advocates of a policy for selective expansion and allowable decline in some small settlements point to the effects of rural depopulation, the growth of commuter villages around towns and cities, and the overall diminution in the old agricultural base for rural settlements as evidence of the need for such action. Probably the greatest problems to be faced are those associated with the population which remains in the more remote areas of the countryside, since shopping, transport, and educational and health facilities must still be provided to at least a minimum standard, even though the decreased population may well make such provisions uneconomic. Chisholm (1962) has suggested that the minimum size for a settlement with a full complement of basic services is around 1,200 people, or about twice the present mean size of small towns and villages. But even this figure may be on the small side. The population within the local market area which is needed for the economic viability of some slightly more specialised services is certainly higher than this, although, of course, the increased mobility seen in several activities, particularly shopping, has effectively increased commercial spheres of influence.

Some reasonably detailed assessments of the minimum population size of the market area necessary for the maintenance of certain services is instructive as it highlights the difficulties which are serious in many rural districts. R. J. Green and J. B. Ayton (1967) have estimated the figures given in Table 25 which are

Service facility	Estimated minimum population
Primary school	at least 5,000
Secondary school	10,000 or more
Three-doctor medical practice	at least 6,000
District nurse	5,000 or more
General purpose grocery shop	1 per 300
Butcher	1 per 2,000
Baker	1 per 3,000
Draper	1 per 2,500
Chemist	1 per 4,000

Table 25. Estimates of the minimum population needed to support certain rural services (after Green and Ayton, 1967)

based on experience in Norfolk. They conclude from their observations that many community services, like schools and medical facilities, require a total population of between 5,000 and 8,000 people to support them, though individual grocery and other shops can exist with far fewer people. Even if allowance is made for increased service mobility, however, many of the smaller villages and hamlets in remote areas are clearly going to be expensive to service from the public purse and run the risk of being neglected by individual commercial concerns.

The problem is not a new one; it was recognised nearly thirty years ago by C. S. Orwin (1944) and has concerned local planning authorities ever since. In some areas, these difficulties of service provision are made even more intractable by other, more localised, causes of rural decay which logically demand a rationalisation of the settlement pattern. This is most clearly seen in the older mining and industrial areas of England and Wales where the decline or disappearance of an economic mainstay such as a coalmine, coupled with a sub-standard social and physical environment for the remaining population, superficially provides a good *prima-facie* case for a rationalisation policy. The actions of the planning authority in East Sussex have also been mentioned in connection with problems of service provision, and there are similar instances, for example, in Devon, Norfolk, Cambridgeshire, Monmouthshire and Durham.

In Norfolk, a policy has been formulated in particularly positive terms. Not only is it suggested that certain main settlements should be preferentially developed to reach a minimum population of 5,000 people, but, at the opposite end of the spectrum, an active policy of service-withdrawal has been advocated in an attempt to hasten the decline of some villages and hamlets (R. J. Green, 1966; Green and Ayton, 1967). Whether such a scheme is really practicable, or even socially justifiable, is a difficult and disputable point. Not unexpectedly, where rationalisation policies have been actively pursued there has often been an unfavourable reaction from the residents involved.

A case in point has occurred in County Durham. The 1951 development plan emphasised the problems of the pit villages in areas of the county where mining was in decline and strongly advocated a policy of population regrouping to provide better living conditions and employment opportunities. Accordingly, the towns and villages in that county were divided into four categories, on the basis of which the future expansion or contraction of individual settlements was to be decided. Seventy such centres were chosen for active growth and a further 143 were to be allowed to continue at about their present size. In 30 settlements, capital investment was to be regulated to allow a gradual decline to take place, while in 114 settlements, later increased to 121, an active policy of assisted contraction was to be followed (J. Barr, 1969). Subsequently, this scheme has been simplified into three groups involving 'growth', 'static' and 'declining' villages (J. R. Atkinson in J. C. Dewdney, ed., 1970). Perhaps not surprisingly, this action has caused much concern and indignation among the residents of the adversely-affected villages. In the short run, there are fears that local services will be drastically curtailed in an attempt to hasten decline; in the long run, there are problems of population resettlement in unfamiliar areas to be faced. On the other hand, the undoubted personal hardships that will be produced must be balanced against the long-term gains in living conditions and environmental quality.

NEW VILLAGES

Where rural population is growing rather than diminishing, the construction of a new village may provide a more satisfactory solution to rural problems than would additional development to some existing settlements, along with the scheduled decline of others. By concentrating as much of the rural development as possible into a new enterprise, it is argued, the problems of infilling and extension which have ruined so many existing settlements are avoided. These contentions are supported by some sociologists, notably R. E. Pahl (1964b). They suggest that any proposals involving, as it were, new wine in old bottles might well be as disastrous from a social viewpoint as from a visual one. Perhaps, then, the best road to rural development should not be in estate-growth alongside the old village, but in a completely fresh start by the construction of entirely new villages where they are needed.

Such a policy is by no means without precedent. The planted towns of the Middle Ages were a conscious attempt to provide an urban base for an expanding local economy (M. W. Beresford, 1967), while, more recently, the new towns of the eighteenth and nineteenth centuries provided what is probably a closer parallel. These later foundations, which were far less sizeable than modern towns, were often the result of philanthropic gestures, coupled with some business foresight which recognised the relationship between labour productivity and living conditions. Many of the examples are well documented (W. Ashworth, 1954): the best-known are probably Titus Salt's small town of Saltaire, dating from the middle of the last century, Robert Owen's developments at New Lanark, the Cadbury settlement at Bournville, Port Sunlight, and the model village at Bromborough Pool on the Wirral (J. N. Tarn, 1965).

In the present century, the few new villages which have been built have perhaps their closest affinity with the modern new towns, rather than with their nineteenth-century counterparts. The influence of the garden city movement has already been mentioned in connection with the later examples of colliery-built villages, and it is seen again in many twentieth century rural developments, particularly in relation to the urban space standards employed. Where it is possible to calculate the land provisions used in planned small settlements, the results provide an interesting sidelight on the social and environmental conditions under which each foundation grew up.

Inevitably, accurate data are lacking for planned small settlements built before the present century, and particularly for the medieval examples. Nevertheless, some indications of space standards are available. For example, the planned settlement of New Woodstock (Oxfordshire) founded by Henry I in 1163 or 1164 seems to have had a total urban area provision of about 22·5 ha/1000p (calculated from details given by R. P. Beckinsale in Beckinsale and Houston, 1968). If this figure can be taken as any true indication, development densities in new, twelfth-century settlements were tigher than is the norm in present-day small settlements (cf. Table 4), but they were very similar to the new towns of the 1950s (Best, 1964). In strong contrast, the new developments in the nineteenth century were often at densities which today would be regarded as totally unacceptable, even though they may have been considered as models of their time when they were first built. By 1871, for example, Saltaire, which the *Manchester Guardian* had hailed as showing 'every improvement that modern art and science have brought to light', had a population of 4,389 persons living at a residential provision of little over 4 ha/1000p (A. Holroyd, 1871). This figure is well below the residential provision recorded for county boroughs in this country at the present time. Such high densities were often made possible by the extremely regular and unimaginative layout employed in the design of many Victorian settlements.

The garden city influence and the general concern with social problems which has grown up in the twentieth century have resulted in a complete change in acceptable rural living standards. This improvement is clearly seen in the few examples of new village development to appear recently in this country. In some places, as at Marks Tey in Essex and Elmswell in Suffolk, very small settlements in areas of growing importance are being expanded to become larger villages. But in at least three locations, at Bar Hill in Cambridgeshire, Studlands Park in Suffolk and New Ash Green in Kent, the villages are completely new creations. Bar Hill village was conceived by the local planning authority as an integral part of the county development plan and has since been developed by private concerns. Building on the site to the north-west of Cambridge started in 1965 and was due for completion in 1971, by which time the settlement was planned to have a total population of about 4,000 people. In the event, these expectations have not been fully attained and construction is still in progress. The village at New Ash Green is again a private undertaking, and building is taking place on a site of 174 ha to the south-west of the Medway towns. The final population will be in the region of 6,000 people. An associated company is also responsible for the construction of Studlands Park, close to Newmarket, which is to have an eventual population of approximately 2,500–3,000.

Planned land provisions in these three small settlements are most interesting as they indicate many of the factors which control rural planning developments in this country. They are recorded in Table 26 which also includes land provisions suggested just after the last war by J. Tyrwhitt (1946) for a new village of about 3,000 people. Although these last proposals were never intended for use on a particular site, their inclusion is justified as they indicate some of the more modern ideas on rural living conditions and complement the data referring to actual new villages.

Small settlement	Popu-lation*	Hous-ing	In-dustry	Open space	Educa-tion	Four main uses	Resi-due	Total urban area
				ha/10³p				
New Ash Green (Kent)	6,000	12·8	–	12·8	–†	25·6	3·4‡	29·0
Bar Hill (Cambs)	5,000	14·5	4·3§	2·0	0·5	21·3	2·5	23·8
Studlands Park (Suffolk)	3,000	10·7	4·2	2·7	0·7	18·3	1·5	19·8
Plan by J. Tyrwhitt (1946)	3,000	19·4	–	5·8	2·7	27·9	1·3	29·2

* Estimated ultimate population
† Land for primary school included under other headings
‡ Commercial land and some small industrial areas
§ A considerable part is scheduled for warehousing and storage

Table 26. The provision of urban land uses in recent new villages (Sources: Cambridgeshire and Isle of Ely County Planning Department, J. Nunn and Sons Ltd., and Bovis – New Homes Division)

Strong contrasts are immediately apparent between these recent proposals and their nineteenth-century counterparts. In particular, overall development densities are now much lower. But bearing in mind that these settlements are envisaged as single, planned units, with all the economies of space allocation which this involves (see Chapter 7), the total land provision of between about 20 and 29 ha/1000p is much closer to that of modern new towns (23·3 ha/1000p) than to the average for small settlements as a whole in this country (34·6 ha/1000p). This situation is reflected particularly in the provision of residential land, where the figures for new villages are similar to or somewhat more liberal than those of new towns, but are only about half the mean provision calculated for small settlements (27·4 ha/ 1000p). The very high provision of open space at New Ash Green (12·8 ha/1000p) is presumably meant to compensate in part for any possible space restrictions within the residential area. In rather the same way, an adjacent golf course is planned at Bar Hill to cover 67·5 ha; and, if included with the open space figure in Table 26, this would give an extremely high provision of 15·5 ha/1000p. These allocations are certainly exceptional and may be partially related to the attempts of the development companies to emphasise the rural nature of the new settlements.

These land provisions clearly indicate the influence of modern concepts of town planning and provide an additional reason for considering these recent new villages as being more closely related to the twentieth-century new towns than to small settlements in general, which frequently possess a far more ancient lineage. A comparison with the land provision figures in Table 6 makes this point clearly enough. Inevitably, like older settlements, these new villages strongly reflect the age in which they are built. Planning policies and procedures in this country have tended to be orientated towards larger urban centres, so that the influence of these towns and cities is mirrored in what at first sight is a rural context. Construction techniques, planned layouts and development densities in both new villages and additions to existing small settlements necessarily have their origins in previous experience in fully urban rather than essentially rural settings.

It is possible to regard recent attitudes to countryside planning and building processes as being merely another indication of the destruction of the older rural order. The decline in agricultural employment, the end of rural isolation with the advent of modern forms of transport, the changeover in the social structure of the village – all these trends have now been joined by a similarity in space standards and design for new building which provides an even closer link between town and country. Consequently, modern developments in rural settlement of all kinds are in process of bringing about an increasing uniformity of appearance which, in all probability, will in time effectively make small towns and villages largely indistinguishable from their truly urban equivalents.

Whether such a process is desirable must remain a matter of opinion. Many would think not; and perhaps it may be fitting that a non-planner should have the last word as a salutory reminder that, however well-intentioned a planning policy may be, this is certainly no assurance that a desirable outcome will always be achieved in the urban countryside. No-one could be more appropriate to provide a final comment than John Betjeman, and a few lines from his poem *The Town Clerk's Views* have a special relevance to the previous discussion:

> '*In a few years this country will be looking*
> *As uniform and tasty as its cooking.*
> *Hamlets which fail to pass the planners' test*
> *Will be demolished. We'll rebuild the rest*
> *To look like Welwyn mixed with Middle West.* . . .
> *We'll keep one ancient village just to show*
> *What England once was when the times were slow –*
> *Broadway for me.* . . .
> *So don't encourage tourists. Stay your hand*
> *Until we've really got the country plann'd.*'

9 · Statistical Summary

An attempt has been made in this book to approach the subject of rural settlement from a very different angle than has been adopted in most previous studies. The frequently attractive and desirable image of the village or small town in the countryside which exists in the minds of most people unfortunately tends to militate against dispassionate evaluation. Yet leaving understandable, if sometimes questionable, emotive attitudes aside, there is in fact no real reason why the small settlement should not be subject to just the same methodical, quantitative dissection that is applied to many of the more populous cities and large towns. Without doubt, such a precise assessment is needed if any soundly-based analysis of small towns and villages is to be carried out, for only in this way can realistic proposals be formulated for their possible futures.

In the previous chapters, therefore, an essentially quantitative appraisal of small settlements has, intentionally, been the procedure adopted. Yet this approach, for all its advantages, contains its own particular dangers. Figures and statistics in this context are only valuable as a means to an end; their use is simply to explain the structure of small towns and villages more fully and more accurately so that information, knowledge and understanding of them are thereby increased. Regrettably, however, the reverse effect can so easily come about with the employment of statistical methods. Far too often, the chief results of such an investigation are submerged in a sea of figures which obscure rather than reveal.

In the present study, a considerable amount of data has been accumulated and presented; and, in the process, it is possible that the main findings may be in prospect of foundering with little trace. Consequently, it has been felt advisable to complete this investigation by looking back over the text and extracting from it the more central and fundamental statistical conclusions. With these items set down in summary form, it is hoped that the reader will then be provided with a comparatively clear-cut skeleton on which the additional and more detailed information, qualifications and comments can be hung.

Accordingly, the main statistical conclusions are as follows:

1. The designation 'small settlements' is a summary term used when referring to places which would frequently be described as small towns and villages. More precisely, this urban category is defined as comprising settlements of under 10,000 population, but excluding isolated dwellings. In the analysis of small settlements, the urban land-use categories adopted have, as far as possible, followed those used for cities and large towns as defined for development plan statistical purposes by the Ministry of Housing and Local Government (now Department of the Environment) (Chapter 2).

2. The main source of data used for the study was cartographic material from the Second Land Utilisation Survey. Supplementary information was provided by development plan statistics for small town map areas and data from a rural settlement survey compiled by the East Sussex County Planning Department. Population figures for small settlements measured from the main data source were obtained from the 1961 Census of Population, with an allowance made for the inhabitants of isolated dwellings. The areal data for small settlements in the Second Land Utilisation Survey were derived from a sample of 30 maps out of the 73 available at the time of study. A stratified random sampling procedure was used so that the conclusions drawn would be statistically valid at a national and regional level (Chapter 2).

3. The predominance of small villages and hamlets in the

166

pattern of rural settlement is very evident. Over half of all the sample settlements have a total area of less than 20 ha, while over a quarter cover less than 8 ha. Altogether, there are of the order of 17,000 small settlements in England and Wales occupying about 285,000 ha of land, or nearly 19 per cent of the whole urban area, and containing some $8\frac{1}{4}$ million inhabitants (Chapter 3).

4. Residential land (including commercial uses) takes up by far the greater part of the total urban area of small settlements: on average, it occupies about 75–80 per cent. Open space is the second most important land use, comprising some 10–15 per cent of the urban area, while industry is relatively insignificant in extent and accounts for no more than 4 per cent (Chapters 4 and 5).

5. Small towns of approximately 7,000 population or over have closer affinities in the composition of their urban area with cities and large towns than with villages. Thus, small town map areas have only 45 per cent of their area under residential use; but this reduction, compared with small settlements in general, is largely matched by an increased percentage of industrial land and a substantially higher proportion of land under the residual uses (25 per cent compared with less than 4 per cent). The contrast is understandable for, by the time a settlement is approaching the upper population limits of the small settlement category, it is beginning to assume the functions associated with larger towns. These are reflected in the growing amount of land provided for transport facilities and public utilities and services, which come under the heading of residual uses (Chapters 4 and 5).

6. The average provision of land (the reciprocal of population density) for the total urban area of small settlements is high (i.e. the density is low). It is calculated as 34·6 ha per thousand population (abbreviated to ha/1000p), but the standard deviation is considerable at 18·1 ha/1000p. The contrast in land provisions, or densities, between each end of the full

urban spectrum is very substantial. In fact, the openness of development in small settlements shown by the figure given above is about twice that found in major towns and cities, or county boroughs (17·5 ha/1000p). With housing alone, the difference is even greater, the figures being 27·4 ha/1000p and 7·6 ha/1000p, respectively (Chapter 4).

7. The evidence from grouped data for various settlement categories indicates that, as the population size of settlement increases, the land provision falls exponentially (i.e. the density of development rises). This general relationship is called the density-size rule. Over the sector of the urban area which comprises small settlements alone, and which is represented by ungrouped Second Land Utilisation Survey data, the rule may be expressed in precise mathematical terms by a least-squares regression model of the form:

$$\log y = 1\cdot9986 - 0\cdot1522 \log x$$
$$\text{where } y = \text{total land provision (ha/1000p)}$$
$$\text{and } x = \text{population of settlement.}$$

A similar mathematical function is obtained with the ungrouped small settlement data for East Sussex. The relationship is perhaps seen and expressed more clearly by the use of the small settlement data grouped according to population size categories. The statistics are, therefore, also presented in this form and equations are derived for residential (and commercial) land and for open space, as well as for the total urban area. The curve representing the density-size rule is clearly not constant over time, and it alters in both slope and position in accordance with changing space standards (Chapter 5).

8. Regional differentiations in the composition and provision of urban land in small settlements are also examined. Little significant regional variation is found in the proportionate composition of the urban area, but, on the other hand, there are strong contrasts in land provisions, or densities. There is, for instance, a notable disparity in this respect between small

settlements in the Highland and Lowland Zones, those in the former zone having far less liberal space standards than those in the latter. For the total urban area, there is a differential of nearly 10 ha/1000p, with the average figure for highland settlements being 28·7 ha/1000p and that for lowland settlements as much as 38·8 ha/1000p. The land provisions for housing alone show a similar divergence at 22·7 and 30·8 ha/1000p, respectively. An analysis of the residuals in the regression model for the size factor strongly confirms these results (Chapter 6).

9. Even greater contrasts in land provision exist between smaller regional groupings of rural settlements. The south and east of England have some very open densities of development, and East Sussex in particular appears to show an extreme form of these conditions with an average provision for the total urban area of 53·2 ha/1000p and for the residential area of 38·7 ha/1000p. In marked contrast, small settlements in the north-east of England have a total urban provision which averages as little as 19·4 ha/1000p, while the figure for housing is no more than 14·7 ha/1000p (Chapter 6).

10. With limited data, an attempt has been made to examine the relationship existing between the local economy, or economic function, of certain types of small settlement and their land-use structure. There appears to be a bias in the location of manufacturing industry towards the Lowland Zone, where industrial sites are recorded in nearly 30 per cent of all small settlements compared with less than half this figure in the Highland Zone settlements. The most common industrial activities classified by standard categories are (a) engineering, shipbuilding and electrical goods, (b) food, drink and tobacco, (c) manufacture of wood and cork, and (d) treatment of non-metalliferous mining products other than coal. Most of these types of manufacturing activity are traditionally associated with rural areas (Chapter 7).

11. The pit village of coal-mining districts provides probably the

most clear-cut example of a functionally orientated small settlement. The 9 mining villages in the national sample have a total urban area provision of only 19·5 ha/1000p, which indicates very tight development for this size of settlement. Conversely, small settlements with a well-developed dormitory function often have a total urban land allocation exceeding 40 ha/1000p, or over 20 per cent more than the mean figure to be expected under the density-size rule (Chapter 7).

12. Within the last half century, the social and economic viability of small settlements has frequently been undermined by rural depopulation. More recently, on the other hand, the growing influx of population from the towns, as commuters, retired people or second-homers, has given new life to some villages in less remote areas of the country. Several planning authorities have adopted policies of selective expansion and allowable decline in regard to small settlements within their counties. There are also a few examples of the construction of completely new villages in recent years. The space standards proposed for these types of new development are between about 20 and 29 ha/1000p for the total urban area. These provisions are much closer to those of modern new towns (an average of 23·3 ha/1000p) than to the generality of small settlements in this country, which are distinctly more open in character (34·6 ha/1000p). New additions to existing villages also tend to follow this same pattern of land provision and design. Consequently, modern developments in rural settlements of all kinds are bringing about an increasing uniformity in appearance between the larger town and the urban countryside (Chapter 8).

Appendix 1 · Hectares/acres conversion table

hectares		acres
0·41	**1**	2·47
2·02	**5**	12·36
4·05	**10**	24·71
6·07	**15**	37·07
8·09	**20**	49·42
10·12	**25**	61·78
12·14	**30**	74·13
14·17	**35**	86·49
16·19	**40**	98·84
18·21	**45**	111·20
20·23	**50**	123·55
22·26	**55**	135·91
24·28	**60**	148·27
26·31	**65**	160·62
28·33	**70**	172·98
30·35	**75**	185·33
32·37	**80**	197·69
34·40	**85**	210·04
36·42	**90**	222·40
38·45	**95**	234·75
40·47	**100**	247·11
44·52	**110**	271·82
48·56	**120**	296·53
52·61	**130**	321·24
56·66	**140**	345·95
60·71	**150**	370·66

The centre column in bold figures represents either of the two columns beside it: e.g. 5 acres = 2·02 ha; 5 ha = 12·36 acres. The table also refers to provisions of land: e.g. 5 acres/1000p = 2·02 ha/1000p.

Appendix 2 · Classification of manufacturing industry in small settlements – Second Land Utilisation Survey

Manufacturing industry as portrayed on the maps of the Second Land Utilisation Survey is classified according to the index numbers of the fourteen main manufacturing categories used in the Industrial Tables volume of the 1951 Census. These are:

 3. Treatment of non-metalliferous mining products
    other than coal (glass, ceramics, cement etc.).   (12)
 4. Chemical and allied trades.   (1)
 5. Metal manufacture.   (3)
 6. Engineering, shipbuilding and electrical goods.   (16)
 7. Vehicles.   (2)
 8. Metal goods, not elsewhere specified.   (3)
 9. Precision instruments, jewellery.   (2)
10. Textiles.   (4)
11. Leather, leather goods and fur.   (0)
12. Clothing.   (5)
13. Food, drink and tobacco.   (15)
14. Manufacture of wood and cork.   (13)
15. Paper and printing.   (2)
16. Other manufacturing industries.   (7)

Figures in brackets record the number of occurrences of a particular industrial category in the small settlements of the sample.

Bibliography

ALLERSTON, P. (1970) 'English village development – findings from the Pickering district of North Yorkshire', *Transactions of the Institute of British Geographers*, 51, 95–109

ALONSO, W. (1960) 'A theory of the urban land market', *Papers and Proceedings of the Regional Science Association*, 6, 149–58

ALONSO, W. (1964) *Location and land use: towards a general theory of land rent*. Harvard University Press, Cambridge, Mass.

ANON. (1966) 'Cambridgeshire: a rural planning policy and its implementation', *Official Architecture and Planning*, 29 (8), 1126–41

ASHWORTH, W. (1954) *The genesis of modern British town planning*. Routledge & Kegan Paul

ATKINSON, J. R. (1958) 'Durham villages and landscape', *The Architects' Journal*, 731–3

AUERBACH, F. (1913) 'Das Gesetz der Bevölkerungskonzentration', *Petermann's Geographische Mitteilungen*, 59, 74–6

BAKER, W. P. (1953) *The English Village*. Oxford University Press

BARLOW REPORT (1940) *Report of the Royal Commission on the distribution of the industrial population*, Cmnd. 6153. H.M.S.O.

BARON, S., ed. (1943) *Country towns in the future England*. Faber and Faber

BARR, J. (1969) 'Durham's murdered villages', *New Society*, 3 April, 523–5

BARTHOLOMEW, H. (1955) *Land uses in American cities*. Harvard University Press, Cambridge, Mass.

BEATH, J. A. (1968) '*A study of the economies of selected rural areas of England and Scotland, with particular reference to the use of the local employment multiplier*', Unpublished M.Phil. thesis, University of London

173

BEAVER, S. H. (1943) *Northamptonshire and Soke of Peterborough*, Parts 58 and 59 of the Report of the Land Utilisation Survey of Britain. Geographical Publications

BECKINSALE, R. P. and J. M. HOUSTON (1968) *Urbanization and its problems: essays presented to E. W. Gilbert*. Basil Blackwell

BERESFORD, M. W. (1967) *New towns of the middle ages*. Lutterworth Press

BERRY, B. J. L., J. W. SIMMONS and R. J. TENNANT (1963) 'Urban population densities: structure and change', *Geographical Review*, 53, 389–405

BEST, R. H. (1957) '*A critical study of the conflicting areal records and estimates of land utilisation in Great Britain since 1900*', Unpublished M.Sc. thesis, University of London

BEST, R. H. (1959) *The major land uses of Great Britain*. Wye College, University of London

BEST, R. H. (1964) *Land for new towns: a study of land use, densities and agricultural displacement*. Town and Country Planning Association

BEST, R. H. (1965) 'Recent changes and future prospects of land use in England and Wales', *Geographical Journal*, 131(1), 1–12

BEST, R. H. (1968a) 'Extent of urban growth and agricultural displacement in post-war Britain', *Urban Studies*, 5(1), 1–23

BEST, R. H. (1968b) 'Competition for land between rural and urban uses', in *Land use and resources: studies in applied geography*, Institute of British Geographers, Special publication No. 1, 89–100

BEST, R. H. (1972) 'March of the concrete jungle', *Geographical Magazine*, 45(1), 47–51

BEST, R. H. and A. G. CHAMPION (1970) 'Regional conversions of agricultural land to urban use in England and Wales, 1945–1967', *Transactions of the Institute of British Geographers*, 49, 15–32

BEST, R. H. and J. T. COPPOCK (1962) *The changing use of land in Britain*. Faber and Faber

BEST, R. H. and J. T. WARD (1956) *The garden controversy*. Wye College, University of London

BOGUE, D. J. (1949) *The structure of the metropolitan community: a study of dominance and subdominance.* University of Michigan

BRACEY, H. E. (1952) *Social provision in rural Wiltshire.* Methuen

BRACEY, H. E. (1962) 'English central villages: identification, distribution and functions', *Lund Studies in Geography,* Series B, Human Geography, 24, 169–90

BRETT, L. (1965) *Landscape in distress.* Architectural Press

BRUCE, M. W. (1967) *'An analysis of changes in urban land use in England and Wales since 1950 from development plan statistics for town map areas',* Unpublished M.Phil. thesis, University of London

BUCHANAN, C. (1962) 'Towns and traffic', *Journal of the Royal Institute of British Architects,* 69 (8), 290–9

BURGESS, E. W. (1925) 'The growth of the city', in *The City,* ed. Park, R. E., E. W. Burgess and R. A. McKenzie, 47–62

CHERRY, G. E. (1969) 'Overcrowding in cities', *Official Architecture and Planning,* 32 (3), 287–90

CHISHOLM, M. (1958) 'Our villages as dormitories', *Town and Country Planning,* 26(5), 195–7

CHISHOLM, M. (1962) 'Have English villages a future?', *Geographical Magazine,* 35, 243–52

CHORLEY, R. J. and P. HAGGETT (1965) *Frontiers in geographical teaching.* Methuen

CHRISTALLER, W. (1933, 1966) *Central Places in Southern Germany,* translated by C. W. Baskin. Prentice-Hall, New Jersey

CLARK, C. (1951) 'Urban population densities', *Journal of the Royal Statistical Society,* Series A. 114, 490–6

CLARK, C. (1967) *Population growth and land use.* Macmillan

CLAWSON, M., R. B. HELD and C. H. STODDARD (1960) *Land for the future.* Johns Hopkins Press, Baltimore

COLEMAN, A. (1961) 'The second land-use survey: progress and prospect', *Geographical Journal,* 127(2), 168–86

COLEMAN, A. and K. R. A. MAGGS (1965) *Land use survey handbook* (4th edition). Second Land Use Survey

COPPOCK, J. T. and H. C. PRINCE, eds. (1964) *Greater London*. Faber and Faber

CULLINGWORTH, J. B. (1960) *Housing needs and planning policy*. Routledge & Kegan Paul

DEFOE, D. (1738) *A tour through the whole island of Great Britain*. (2nd edition)

DEWDNEY, J. C. (1970) *Durham County and City with Teesside*. British Association

DICKINSON, R. E. (1932) 'The distribution and functions of the smaller urban settlements of East Anglia', *Geography*, 17, 19–31

DICKINSON, R. E. (1934) 'The town plans of East Anglia: a study in urban morphology', *Geography*, 19, 37–50

EVERSON, J. A. and B. P. FITZGERALD (1969) *Settlement patterns*. Longmans

GALSWORTHY, J. (1906) *The man of property*. Penguin Books edition, 1951

GREEN, C. M. (1966) *The rise of urban America*. Hutchinson

GREEN, R. J. (1966) 'The remote countryside', *Planning Outlook*, N.S. I. 17–37

GREEN, R. J. (1971) *Country planning: the future of the rural regions*. Manchester University Press

GREEN, R. J. and J. B. AYTON (1967) 'Changes in the pattern of rural settlement', in *Report of the Town Planning Institute Conference* 'Planning for the changing countryside'

HAGGETT, P. (1965) *Locational analysis in human geography*. Edward Arnold

Hampshire County Council (1966) *Village life in Hampshire*

HARRIS, C. D. and E. L. ULLMAN (1945) 'The nature of cities', *Annals of the American Academy of Political and Social Science*, 242, 7–17

HOLROYD, A. (1871) *Saltaire and its founder*

HOSKINS, W. G. (1955) *The making of the English landscape*. Hodder

HOSKINS, W. G. and L. D. STAMP (1963) *The common lands of England and Wales*. Collins

HOYT, H. (1939) *The structure and growth of residential neighbour-*

hoods in American cities. United States Federal Housing Administration

HUNT, A. J., ed. (1968) 'Population maps of the British Isles, 1961', *Transactions of the Institute of British Geographers*, 43

JACKSON, V. J. (1968) *Population in the countryside: growth and stagnation in the Cotswolds*. Frank Cass

JAY, L. S., K. D. FINES and J. FURMIDGE (1965) 'Village planning in East Sussex', *University of Pennsylvania Law Review*, 114(1), 106–26

JOHNSON, J. H. (1967) *Urban geography: an introductory analysis*. Pergamon Press

KING, G. (1696/1802) *Statistical account of the state and condition of England and Wales in 1696*. (published 1802)

LASLETT, P. (1965) *The world we have lost*. Methuen

MANDELKER, D. R. (1962) *Green belts and urban growth: English town and country planning in action*. University of Wisconsin Press

MASSER, F. I. and D. C. STROUD (1965) 'The metropolitan village', *Town Planning Review*, 36(2), 111–24

MEITZEN, A. (1895) *Siedelung und Agrarwesen der Westgermanen und Ostgermanen*

Ministry of Agriculture, Fisheries and Food (1968) *A century of agricultural statistics: Great Britain 1866-1966*. H.M.S.O.

Ministry of Housing and Local Government (1955) *Town and Country Planning Act, 1947 – First review of approved development plans*, Circular No. 9/55. H.M.S.O.

Ministry of Housing and Local Government (1959) *Annual Report, 1958*, Cmnd. 737, Appendix XXII. H.M.S.O.

Ministry of Housing and Local Government (1967) *Settlement in the countryside*. H.M.S.O.

ORWIN, C. S. (1944) *Countryside planning*. Oxford University Press

ORWIN, C. S. (1945) *Problems of the countryside*. Cambridge University Press

PAHL, R. E. (1964a) 'The two-class village', *New Society*, 27 February, 7–9

PAHL, R. E. (1964b) 'The old and the new: a case study', *New Society*, 29 October, 10–12

PAHL, R. E. (1965a) *Urbs in rure: the metropolitan fringe in Hertfordshire*. London School of Economics

PAHL, R. E. (1965b) 'Class and community in English commuter villages', *Sociologia Ruralis*, V(1), 5–23

PAHL, R. E. (1966) 'The social objectives of village planning', *Official Architecture and Planning*, 29(8), 1146–50

PETERS, G. H. (1962) 'Industrial development in country towns', *Town and Country Planning*, 30(10), 386–9

ROBERTSON, I. M. L. (1961) 'The occupational structure and distribution of rural population in England and Wales', *Scottish Geographical Magazine*, 77, 165–79

ROBINSON, M. (1963) 'The north Cotswolds', *Town and Country Planning*, 31(4), 177–83

ROGERS, A. W. (1969) '*A quantitative study of the existing structure and provisions of land use in small settlements in England and Wales*', Unpublished M.Phil. thesis, University of London

ROSTOW, W. W. (1960) *The stages of economic growth: a non-communist manifesto*. Cambridge University Press

SAMUEL COMMISSION (1925) *Royal Commission on the coal industry*. H.M.S.O.

SAVILLE, J. (1957) *Rural depopulation in England and Wales – 1851–1951*. Routledge & Kegan Paul

SCOTT REPORT (1942) *Report of the committee on land utilisation in rural areas*, Cmnd. 6378. H.M.S.O.

SHARP, T. (1946) *The anatomy of the village*. Penguin Books

SMAILES, A. E. (1946) 'The urban mesh of England and Wales', *Transactions of the Institute of British Geographers*, 11, 87–101

SMITH, R. D. P. (1968) 'The changing urban hierarchy', *Regional Studies*, 2(1), 1–19

STAFFORD, H. A. (1963) 'The functional bases of small towns', *Economic Geography*, 39, 165–75

STAMP, L. D. (1962) *The land of Britain: its use and misuse*. Longmans

TARN, J. N. (1965) 'The model village at Bromborough Pool', *Town Planning Review*, 35(4), 329–36

THOMPSON, F. (1945) *Lark Rise to Candleford*. Oxford University Press

THORBURN, A. (1971) *Planning villages*. Estates Gazette

THORPE, H. (1949) 'The green villages of county Durham', *Transactions of the Institute of British Geographers*, 15, 153–80

TYRWHITT, J. (1946) *Planning and the countryside*. Art and Educational Publications

VINING, R. (1955) 'A description of certain spatial aspects of an economic system', *Economic Development and Cultural Change*, 3, 147–95

WATSON, J. W. and J. B. SISSONS (1964) *The British Isles: a systematic geography*. Nelson

WELLER, J. (1967) *Modern agriculture and rural planning*. Architectural Press

WHITE, P. H. (1951) '*A critical analytical account of recent urban development in coal mining areas in Great Britain*', Unpublished M.Sc. thesis, University of London

WHITEHAND, J. W. R. (1967) 'The settlement morphology of London's cocktail belt', *Tijdschrift voor Economische en Sociale Geografie*, 58, 20–7

WIBBERLEY, G. P. (1960) 'Changes in the structure and functions of the rural community', *Sociologia Ruralis*, 1(2), 118–27

WIBBERLEY, G. P. (1965) 'The changing role of the country town', in *Festskrift til K. K. Skovgaard*, 135–42

WIBBERLEY, G. P. (1967) 'The disappearance of rural Britain', *The Bledisloe lecture, Royal Agricultural College, Cirencester*, September 1967

WOODS, K. S. (1968) *Development of country towns in the southwest midlands during the 1960's*. (mimeo). Oxford University, Institute for Research in Agricultural Economics

ZIPF, G. K. (1949) *Human behaviour and the principle of least effort*. Addison-Wesley Press, Cambridge, Mass.

Index